Blank Page to First Draft in 15 Minutes

The most effective shortcut to
preparing a speech or presentation

Phillip Khan-Panni

communicators

Published by How To Books Ltd,
3 Newtec Place, Magdalen Road,
Oxford OX4 1RE. United Kingdom.
Tel: (01865) 793806. Fax: (01865) 248780
email: info@howtobooks.co.uk
http://www.howtobooks.co.uk

First edition 2001

British Library Cataloguing in Publication Data.
A catalogue record for this book is available from the British Library.

Edited by Nikki Read
Cover design by Baseline Arts Ltd, Oxford

Produced for How To Books by Deer Park Productions
Typeset and design by Baseline Arts Ltd, Oxford
Printed and bound in Great Britain

NOTE: The material contained in this book is set out in good faith for general
guidance and no liability can be accepted for loss or expense incurred as a result
of relying in particular circumstances on statements made in this book. Laws
and regulations are complex and liable to change, and readers should check the
current position with the relevant authorities before making personal
arrangements.

Communicators is an imprint of How To Books.

Contents

5 Mining Your Brain for Usable Content

This chapter is about brainstorming: what it means, how to do it, and why it is a powerful technique for extracting usable content from the recesses of your own mind. Here you'll find no less than 50 ideas for a speech on How to Make a Speech That People Will Want to Hear.

6 Simple Structures to Develop Your Arguments

The key to successful communication, when you make a speech or presentation, is structure, and in this chapter you will find guidance on how to avoid being a ship without a rudder, when you speak in public, plus five simple structures that you can use at any time.

7 Fit Your Content to the Structure

This is one of the most practical chapters in the book. Step by step, it shows you how to create a template and fit your selected ideas together, using the 50 ideas from the brainstorming in Chapter 5, and ending up with a set of speaker's notes or, alternatively, a mind map of the sample speech.

8 First Draft Speech from Speaker's Notes

The speech itself! Based on the brainstormed ideas in Chapter 5, the structure, template and speaker's notes in Chapter 7, here's how the final speech might look, complete with subheads and transitions. The purpose of this draft text is to show how the techniques in this book can work in practice. Note the 'spoken' style of language, and the rhetorical devices.

9 When You Need to be Succinct   104

How relevant is this book to your own situation? This chapter covers 13 situations when it pays to be succinct, and when to use the techniques and disciplines detailed in this book. And 13 different kinds of occasion when you need to be able to put your case clearly and to the point.

10 When You Have More Time   113

Are these techniques useful only when you are in a hurry? Clearly not. And in this chapter you will find the unique AMBER formula for proper preparation, to ensure that you connect with every member of your audience, achieve the right focus and avoid reliance on technology. Plus some valuable advice on how to speak so others want to listen.

11 Checklist   126

Finally, here's a checklist to consult for each important ingredient in your talk, as a quick reference and reminder of the essentials. In a way, this provides a summary of the main points of the entire book, covering everything from the message and the structure, to the benefits and the outcome, as well as visual aids, other equipment and even delivery. Plus a summary of the 15-minute preparation that is the core of this book.

Preface

In my training programmes on presentation skills, the two topics which people find most useful are Structure and Blank Page to First Draft. In particular, they say they like the magic formula for preparing a working outline in a short time. Hence this book.

However, the inevitable question must be: why write an entire book on a formula that could be explained in a few pages? The answer is that the 'formula' on its own is not enough, because you could end up with a one-off presentation that will get you out of trouble on one occasion, but take you no further. My purpose is to help you to understand the processes that will enable you not only to marshal your thoughts constructively, but also to fashion those thoughts into messages that others will want to hear.

In dealing with Structure I have also sought to make it easier for you to speak off the cuff, by applying one of the simple structures you will find in Chapter 6. All the techniques in this book will help you to communicate more succinctly, in informal as well as in formal situations.

It is a book you can read from start to finish, or dip into at will. I have tried to make each section self-sufficient, so that you do not have to rummage through several sections to give you the answers you need. You will therefore find certain points covered in more than one place. And although the main purpose of the book is to help you put your presentation together, you will also find quite a few tips on putting it across.

The book's underlying purpose is to help you prepare quickly, yet produce presentations that will engage the attention and interest of your listeners. I urge you not to fly by the seat of your pants. It's not worth the risk. With a little practice, you will be able to apply the techniques in this book to go from blank page to a usable first draft in about 15 minutes.

It should help you to speak in public without fear, and in a way that makes others want to listen.

Phillip Khan-Panni

To Sylvia Milton
who first encouraged me to write this book

Chapter 1

Don't even think of busking it

In this Chapter:

♦ **when the deadline is upon you, with nothing prepared ...**

♦ **... or when you've been given no notice**

♦ **why it's fatal to attempt to 'busk it'**

♦ **what makes a presenter boring**

♦ **the terror of the blank page**

♦ **the confidence from knowing how.**

The hardest part of preparing a speech or presentation is the blank sheet of paper. Where to start? Is there a simple formula that will get you started and out of trouble?

There is, and this book will provide it for you. However, it is not enough to give you the formula because, no matter how effective it might be, if you follow it slavishly, all your presentations will seem the same and even you will be bored by them.

My purpose is to provide you with a method – not just a formula – some technique for assembling your ideas and focusing on your core message, so that your communication works. You should always aim to enable your listeners to carry away a clear understanding of your message, such that would enable them to summarize it in a sentence or two if someone asked them, 'What was that presentation about?'

Central to that process is *structure*, and I deal with that in detail in Chapter 7. Structure helps you to communicate concisely – and be understood more easily. It helps the speaker to transmit and the listener to receive.

Coping with tight deadlines

Have you ever found yourself in the position of having to deliver a presentation the next day (or even later that same day) with nothing prepared? Or of being asked to make a presentation at very short notice? Ever been faced with that dreaded request to 'Say a few words'?

Most senior managers have been in that position at some time, and a few cope brilliantly. Most of us, however, find the prospect terrifying, and it's hardly surprising. Just imagine yourself standing up to present with nothing prepared:

> You are confident that you know your stuff, but as the moment of truth is upon you, you suddenly doubt your ability to make an opening impact ... the devastating wit that you expected to arrive seems to have got lost in transit ... the scattered ideas you thought you could fashion into a message of

breathtaking impressiveness now seem
shallow and inadequate ... and you can just
picture your peers and seniors sitting with
their arms crossed, frowning with
disapproval.

That's when you know you *should* have prepared or,
better still, fallen under a convenient bus on the way to
work that day.

Tight deadlines have a way of turning your collar into a
tight noose. Sometimes you may get away with it. More
often you do not, even if you think you did. Why take
the risk?

The *coping strategies* I have observed include the following
(tick any that might apply to you):

- ❑ apologizing for lack of preparation
- ❑ brief and inarticulate offerings followed
  by embarrassed silence and surrender
- ❑ rambling through every aspect of the
  topic until at last a focus is found
- ❑ self-deprecating humour in an effort to
  win the sympathy vote
- ❑ energetically attacking the subject and
  the occasion as though it were a test of
  virility
- ❑ using the occasion to demonstrate an
  encyclopaedic knowledge of the subject
- ❑ basking in the limelight and going on
  forever.

There are others, of course, and no doubt you have developed your own. The point is, how well does it work ... for the audience? Busking it is a dangerous strategy. The chances of failure are extremely high, not only because few people have the talent to speak brilliantly off the cuff, but also because a speaker's lack of preparation is usually evident, and that gives offence to the audience.

After all, would you pay to hear your own unprepared talk?

Coping with impromptu speaking

Only the other day, in a Masterclass I was running, we had a session on impromptu speaking. In order to discover the level of skill of the delegates, and to see how they would select their material, I asked a couple of them to talk about quite large topics, such as 'London Transport'. One of the delegates, a lady in a very senior job, rose and fixed her eyes on the blank screen behind me, then launched into a flood of words that had nothing whatever to do with the topic she'd been given.

She was articulate, she had a good voice, and her vocabulary was of a high standard. She looked good, and she had personal presence which she had developed in a previous career as a schoolteacher. But as a piece of communication it failed, and I gained two insights during her mini speech. The first was about her coping strategy, and the second was about one of the other delegates.

Her coping strategy was to impress her audience with her fluency and authority in her voice and manner, much as she might have done when she was teacher, dealing with children who have neither the knowledge nor the self-assurance to say, 'Please miss, what exactly is the point you are making?' The motivation behind her strategy was to avoid being seen as inadequate, so she switched into competitive mode and overwhelmed us with her flood of words.

Teachers are experienced at talking at length and filling the time slot from beginning to end. Their audiences, being schoolchildren, cannot get up and leave. Nor are they likely to criticize the teacher's performance. So the teacher can get away with irrelevancies, limited content and indifferent delivery. Not so in business life, as this lady found out when she received her feedback.

Preparing on the run

Now, while she was speaking, one of the other delegates was engrossed in his laptop. In fact, he was typing away. All the delegates had been asked to bring with them a short presentation, complete with appropriate visual aids, which they were to present to camera. This particular chap had prepared nothing. He was preparing his presentation during the training session, while attention was on someone else.

How effective do you suppose his presentation was? Well, at best it can only have been a re-hash of something he had done before. It is hard to be original when you cannot give your preparation all your attention and concentration. He was preparing on the run.

Have you ever been in a similar position? Ever had to cobble together some thoughts during the early items on the agenda, hoping that the Chairperson wouldn't ask you a question? And if so, was it the best performance of which you were capable?

Preparing on the run can work if you know how. With the right formula, you can produce a working outline in just 15 minutes – as this book will demonstrate.

Tale of two talks

I once knew a chap (let's call him Henry) who was renowned as a speaker in his circle. Henry was fluent, well-spoken, and had an enviable command of the English language. So it was natural that a close friend of his should ask Henry to be Best Man at his wedding. Unfortunately, Henry didn't take the assignment very seriously, and he neglected to prepare a proper Best Man's speech. If you have ever been a Best Man, you will know that it is not an easy task. Henry remained sanguine until the day of the wedding.

He then asked me what he should include in his speech. I rattled off some of the essential ingredients, but I could see that Henry's interest was wandering. When it was his turn to get on his feet, he failed to connect with his audience. He announced that he was going to open with a joke, but the joke he chose was feeble and inappropriate. It not only failed to raise a giggle, it actually gave offence to some of the more conservative guests.

In show business terms, he 'died' on his feet. It was embarrassing and it deeply disappointed the groom and those others who'd had high expectations of Henry's speech. It took Henry many years to live down that disaster, and he was never again asked to be Best Man.

How this book came about

On another occasion, I attended a meeting of my branch of Toastmaster International, only to be asked by the club President if I would fill one of the speaking slots, because one of the speakers on the programme had failed to turn up.

I retired to a quiet corner for ten minutes and produced a speech outline. The speech I gave, which was almost impromptu, won the award for Best Speech of the evening. Sylvia Milton, who was there with me, later said, 'What was most impressive about that was the way you threw something together so quickly, yet made it sound so well prepared. Why don't you analyze how you did that and teach it to others? You could even put it in a book.'

This is that book. And it is dedicated to Sylvia.

The difference between my experience and Henry's was that I had a formula to follow. Henry didn't. He thought he could charm his way through the assignment, treating it as amplified conversation. That's a common mistake, and it means that the speaker doesn't really care about his or her audience.

Not to prepare usually means you don't respect your listeners. And if you don't respect them you cannot expect an encouraging response. Your attitude will communicate itself to them, and you are more likely to encounter hostility.

The first lesson, therefore, is to develop the right attitude to your prospective audience. Take the occasion seriously, be prepared to make the effort, and apply the disciplines that this book will provide. There is a short-cut at the end, but it would be in your own best interests to read the whole book before applying the formula, because it is not enough to know what works – it helps to understand *why* it works.

What makes a good speaker?

In a companion volume in this series (*2-4-6-8, How Do You Communicate?*) I discuss more fully what exactly it takes to be a speaker. Let me give you a brief summary of the essential qualities, to underscore why you should never consider busking it, when you have a serious speech to deliver.

When people ask me what it takes to be a speaker, I reply: three things. They are the Three Ms – Message, Messenger, Method.

- ◆ **Message:** Have something to say.
- ◆ **Messenger:** It must belong to you and you must really want to say it.
- ◆ **Method:** Finally, develop the skills to put it across in a meaningful way.

Have you noticed how articulate and fluent you can be when you are angry about some injustice or poor service? That's because you have something to say. Notice how impassioned your delivery is when you are in that frame of mind? That's because you really want to say what's on your mind. And yet, even in the midst of your passion you may sometimes wish you had greater skill in putting your point across and persuading your listeners to your point of view. That's because you recognize the value of *technique* in making the communication effective.

Although your 'speech' may be impromptu when your blood is up, you are not winging it. You are saying what you believe and what you know. It's an expression of your existing beliefs. You are therefore speaking from knowledge, and as an expert in the opinions you are expressing. That's what gives you conviction and authority.

The same should be true of your prepared speeches. Even when you have little time to prepare, use that time. Follow the guidelines in this book and you will be more prepared than you ever thought possible in the short time available. It will enable you to sound more authoritative, better informed and confident.

If it's true that 'the old ones are the best', bear in mind this ancient piece of advice:

◆ *Proper planning prevents pretty poor performance.*

In summary ...

◆ **Recognize the coping strategy you use when faced with a looming deadline.**

◆ **Never plan to give a performance that's less than your best.**

◆ **You can be properly prepared even in a few minutes.**

◆ **Busking it can expose you to disaster.**

◆ **Retain your respect for your audience – they'll sense it if you don't.**

◆ **Remember the Three Ms that make a speaker worth hearing: Message, Messenger, Method.**

Chapter 2

What shall I talk about?

In this Chapter:

◆ **relevance to the occasion**

◆ **relevance to the audience**

◆ **what are the expectations of the audience?**

◆ **who is the audience?**

◆ **what are you speaking?**

◆ **why is it *you*, and what is your expertise?**

Choosing what to talk about

One of the hardest tasks facing a professional speaker is Choice of Topic. Some speakers agonize over it for years, altering and re-altering their standard speeches as they seek to define and then refine their expertise.

There is a similar problem when preparing an occasional speech or presentation. The temptation is to collect a pile of books and other reference material in the hope of finding nuggets of inspiration or interesting ideas that you can adopt, adapt, improve. Hours later, you'll probably find yourself preparing to write a thesis or learned dissertation on the subject.

Three words of advice: **don't do it.**

Two reasons for the advice:

1   Reference books and other secondhand materials are the wrong starting place. Better to look inside yourself.
2   It's a mistake to try and make your speech or presentation the definitive statement on the subject.

Have confidence in your own expertise

> An expert is a fellow who is afraid to learn anything new because then he wouldn't be an expert anymore. **Harry S Truman, US President**

The reason you are making the speech or presentation is because of your personal expertise, (real or otherwise) or because you are considered an authority on the subject, by virtue of your knowledge or your position. People will want to hear what makes you that authority, not what you can distill from books. They can do the research just as well themselves.

What's *your* take on the subject? What's your angle, what's the filter you place on the facts that will tell your audience what *you* think about the facts or arguments you present, and what you want *them* to think.

First, the general principle: look inside yourself and understand that your listeners want to know what you know. They want to know what you think about what you know. They want to know what they should think about what you tell them.

Do you know that you know?

> He who knows not and knows not that he
> knows not is a fool—shun him,
> He who knows not and knows that he
> knows not is a child—teach him,
> He who knows and knows not that he
> knows is asleep—wake him,
> He who knows and knows that he knows is
> wise—follow him.

Don J Unwin

It is important to know *what* you know, and it is wise to know *that* you know. That may sound quaint, but consider the logic: how easy is it for you to claim that you are an expert on any subject? Let's suppose you could persuade yourself that you are an expert, would you be prepared to go on television right now, this very minute, and sit on a panel of experts on that subject, or be interviewed by one of the Dimbleby brothers? Could you do it?

If not, why not? Most people would at least hesitate, more because they did not feel confident in their knowledge than through fear of the camera. A typical reaction would be, 'What if I didn't know the answers to the questions I was asked?' Or what if they just didn't know enough. And yet, take away the pressure of being a panel expert, sit them down in front of a panel of other experts, and they will soon start thinking, 'I know just as much as they do.'

We all know more than we think we do. The problem for speakers is in deciding on which topic we can parade ourselves as experts. On which subjects can we speak with authority and put across a point of view that is both interesting and well-founded. Have you decided on your own topic or topics? Here's where you need to start thinking of yourself as a specialist – the person that others would turn to for advice, guidance or instruction.

Are you speaking for you or for your audience?

Relevance is a vital factor: how relevant is your topic to the audience and to the occasion? It's incredible how often such an obvious consideration is forgotten or overlooked.

It was certainly overlooked when a certain public speaking organization held a video-ing day for members. Because professional speakers need videos to demonstrate their talents, the organization put on an event in which a succession of speakers delivered 15 minutes of their best material to an audience of their peers, with a full film crew in attendance.

Unfortunately, there were three large problems:

1   There was **no common theme**, since all the speakers determined their own content. The result was an unbalanced programme that left the audience punch drunk well before the end.

2   The speakers were **not all of a consistently high standard**, which meant that the audience felt the whole event was sub-standard. They also felt that the event had been staged for the benefit of the speakers, and not for those who had paid to attend.

3   Most importantly, several of the speeches were **directed at AN audience rather than to THAT audience.**

Neither the organizers of the event nor most of the speakers had stopped to consider the needs or expectations of the audience. Had it been an invited audience, there would have been no problem. But this audience had paid to be there. Not only that, they had come looking for some professional benefit, some knowledge or techniques that would help them with their own careers as speakers.

This is an extreme example, but the same considerations apply to every meeting and to every speaker preparing a speech: make it relevant to the audience and to the occasion.

Why is it you?

In Chapter 1 I said there were three essentials for a speaker: **Message, Messenger, Method.** Let's now consider the expectations of the audience, and how they relate to the speaker's three Ms.

What would prompt you to attend if you received a leaflet about a talk or presentation? Top of most people's list would be the subject matter of the talk. Next, it would be the credentials of the speaker. Third, it would be the speaker's skill or reputation as an orator. Do you agree?

1 **Subject matter.** Isn't that the thing that first engages your interest? You ask yourself, 'What's this about? Is it relevant to me? Do I need to know this?' And then you decide to read more about the talk.
2 **Credentials.** Next you consider the speaker, don't you? You ask yourself, 'Is this person an expert in the subject, someone who could tell me things I don't know, but need to know?'
3 **Skill.** Sometimes it may be enough to know that the speaker is an Anthony Robbins or a Les Brown, to persuade you to book up for the talk, because they have established their reputations as speakers with messages that you want to hear, and the credentials to speak with authority on their subject, and most of all that they have a speaking style that you know will excite, motivate and inspire you.

- The Subject Matter is WHAT is being said.
- The speaker's Credentials are WHO is speaking.
- The Skill indicates HOW it will be said.

Looked at another way:
- WHAT is being said is the **Message**.
- WHO is saying it is the **Messenger**.
- HOW it is being said in the **Method**.

So you see, the three essentials for a speaker must match the three expectations of an audience.

But how is that relevant to choosing your theme? Simply this: it's not enough to deliver evidence of your expertise. Don't drown your listeners in facts and information. Don't try to impress them with your expertise. Instead, let them hear your point of view. Look within yourself for a message that belongs to you, yet which might be of relevance and significance for your listeners.

The first question you need to answer is, 'Why is it you that has been asked to speak?'

The answer isn't, Because I'm the Managing Director or Because it's my project. The answer should be, Because I can tell them something that they don't already know, and which they will want to know.

Let's now consider how you can go about choosing your theme for your speech or presentation.

Choosing your theme

You already know the broad subject of your talk. What you need to decide is the specific aspect of that subject that you are going to address. The temptation will be to attempt to produce the complete guide to the subject in half an hour. It cannot be done. Don't try to write the encyclopedia on the subject. Don't even try to give your listeners enough information to make them experts by the time you have stopped speaking. It can't be done, and it is an unreasonable expectation.

How long did it take you to become the expert that you are? Days, weeks, months, years? It is possible to turn your listeners into similar experts in the short time it takes to complete your talk? Clearly not.

So what should you be doing? You should be trying to identify a single message that will bring about some change in the thinking, attitude or behaviour of your audience. I say a 'single message' because a more complex text will impose on your audience the responsibility to interpret your message and work out its relevance to them, and how they might apply it to their own circumstances. That is also an unreasonable expectation. They won't do it.

How to focus your mind on your purpose

Understand your role. It is not to prove yourself an expert with every conceivable fact at your command. It is to offer them a new outlook on a topic of mutual interest, and something that they can take away and put to use immediately. Start by asking yourself these five questions:

1 Why am I presenting?
2 Why should they listen to me?
3 What can I offer that someone else cannot?
4 What (change) do I want my speech/presentation to achieve?
5 What can they apply right away?

Those five questions will help you to focus your mind on why it is you who is giving the talk, and what you can offer. You need to understand and believe in your own expertise.

Now turn your attention to your subject, and ask yourself these new questions:

1 What angle or slant on the subject can I offer that's different and better?
2 What makes me an expert on the subject?
3 Why do I want to tell them whatever it is that I propose to say?
4 How is it relevant to the audience?
5 What are their expectations?
6 What would be the result if they ignored what I said, and do I care?

A character in the P.G. Wodehouse novels used to say 'You've got to have a Nangle.' So what's *your* Nangle? Simply to present your facts straight up can be very boring, and not much better than presenting it in writing. If all you communicate is facts, why not allow your listeners to read the research for themselves and make up their own minds on the meaning of the information? Save your time and theirs by putting your information on one side of a small piece of paper and sending it to your audience!

However, if you want to make the speech or presentation, you need to consider what is special about the information you are putting across. You need to be clear about your take on it. You need to place your personal filter over it so that your listeners hear more than the information alone: they hear *your* interpretation of it. That's what makes it worth hearing.

Now suppose your starting point is a blank sheet of paper, and you are trying to develop a topic, perhaps because you want to offer yourself to the speaking circuit. In such a circumstance, the rules are similar, but Step One is different.

Remember that you should make speeches or presentations only on subjects you know thoroughly. Your credibility rests on your perceived expertise. So start by asking yourself what you are good at.

- ◆ What do you know a lot about?
- ◆ What can you do that others cannot?
- ◆ What do have a passion for or about?
- ◆ Would you pay to hear you speak?

In summary ...

- ◆ **Look inside yourself to discover what to talk about.**
- ◆ **Always make it relevant to your listeners and to the occasion.**
- ◆ **Don't try to be comprehensive: be selective.**
- ◆ **Remember the Three Ms: Message / Messenger / Method.**
- ◆ **Develop an angle on the subject.**
- ◆ **Understand your role as 'interpreter' of the information you present.**

Chapter 3

The importance of a sexy title

In this Chapter:

◆ **you must 'sell' your talk**

◆ **what would cause you to attend such a talk?**

◆ **remember WIIFM**

◆ **examples of boring titles**

◆ **difference between facts or features and benefit.**

Some time ago I was invited to assist in an international conference which was called something like: *'Sustainable Quality Tourism and Associated Infrastructure Development'*. When I was first told the title I thought it was a joke and started to laugh. But the conference organizer just asked me what was so funny.

I said, 'Is that really the title of the event?'

She replied, 'Yes. That's what the event is all about.'

Me: 'Are you seriously expecting people to come to an event with a title that is not only very long, but is full of b-o-r-i-n-g words like Infrastructure?'

Her: 'Why not? The title describes what the event is about. What's wrong with that?'

Me: 'It doesn't do anything to sell the event or make it sound attractive or appealing. Why leave people to decide if this is for them or not. Why not help them to make the decision to attend by including something sexy?'

Her: 'But all my conferences have similar titles.'

Me: 'Show me.'

She then handed me a document headed, *'Alternative Methods of Financing for Local Authorities and Municipalities'.* I groaned.

What was interesting was that she could not see that the titles were not only unappealing, they were actually turn-offs. Certain words like 'Municipalities' can have associations of teeth-grinding boredom. Such titles are as inspiring as the index of a dictionary. They contain no benefits, they do not contain words with sparkling or attractive associations.

Contrast those titles with the following:

- What's New in Performance Management?
- Effective Communication Strategies
- Developing a Learning Strategy
- 2-4-6-8, How Do You Communicate?
- Using Psychology to Understand Teamwork

- Getting the right performance out of the wrong people
- The key secrets of being an entrepreneur
- How to be an Entrepreneur and Keep Your Day Job
- Cross culture: Eagle or Vulture?
- Motivation: Mind Over Matter
- From Blank Page to First Draft in 15 minutes.

Some of those titles will appeal more to you than others, mainly because of their relevance to your own interests or needs at this time. They will appeal at all because they contain benefits, some explicit, some implicit. The more specific the benefit the more likely it is to either appeal or not appeal. If the benefit is vague or general, you 'might' be interested, depending on your mood or whatever else is on offer.

Importance of a sexy title

The obvious question is:
- Does the title matter?

To answer that question properly, we should take a moment to consider how people (including ourselves) respond to messages. The two most important considerations are personal interest and ease of understanding.

Take personal interest. As you know, everyone's favourite radio station is WII FM, which stands for What's In It For Me? A title, headline or message will grab and hold your attention only if it signals relevance and benefit to you. If you have no interest in the subject, you'll turn away saying, 'That's not for me'. If you hate anything to do with accountancy, for example, not even the sexiest title for a talk on managing your money will turn you on, beyond possibly passing it on to your own accountant.

However, if the topic *is* of interest to you, it still has to be sold to you. I'm sure you know the difference between features and benefits. A feature is just a characteristic, the benefit is the way that characteristic helps you.

Here's a *feature-laden* title:

◆ *Tailored Market Information Report on interested companies in Norway*

Here's a *benefit-laden* alternative:

◆ *The Norwegian companies that most want to do business with you*

The first version simply describes the report. It is therefore likely to be put on one side and not read until the last moment. The second interprets the value to the company, and is therefore more likely to get immediate attention. If you had two reports, with those two titles, which would you rather read – and why?

The first, which was actually the title of a report I received, is as inspiring as a telephone directory. Its author either did not stop to consider what might be of interest to me in the report, or he did not care. Either way, it scored low marks with me. The second, which is the alternative I offered him later, identifies the key benefit: hot prospects for me to contact.

Let your title work as hard as an Ad Headline

Press advertisements rely on their headlines to identify their target audience and stop them in their tracks. The headlines scream, 'Stop! This is for YOU!' Here are some examples:

LOANS: **Borrow £20,000 for just £187 a month.**
WATCH: **Retail price £379. On your wrist £79. In your pocket £300.**
MORTGAGES: **With Halifax Mortgages, start low and stay low.**
INSURANCE: **If you knew how much you're being overcharged for life cover, the shock could kill you.**
CRUISES: **Condensed seven day break: Just add water.**

It is by no means the norm to have benefit headlines like those above. In fact I had to search for them in several magazines and newspapers, but these are the kinds of advertisements that would get my attention, unlike the self-satisfied variety that simply declare, 'Look at me!'

Apart from presentations that you have to attend because of your job, no one can persuade you to attend a talk or presentation unless they first capture your attention with a title that signals it relevance and benefit to you. Suppose you work in Marketing and you receive a mailing about a seminar called *'Marketing'*. Would you go? The title is relevant, but is it exciting and is it enough?

On the other hand, suppose you had been in a dead-end job, and were made redundant. How would you feel about an invitation to a seminar called, *'How to be fully qualified for a career in IT and job ready in 6 months'*?

Titles are important. They act in the same way as headlines, and the same rules apply. Their role is to attract the relevant audience and offer a compelling reason to accept or at least to find out more. They tell your audience why they should be there and what to expect. And they encourage you to focus on what you are offering them.

Here's how to write your title

The first thing to decide is the MAIN BENEFIT of your talk. What exactly will your listeners gain by attending and sitting through the talk? Even if the talk is an in-house one, for colleagues or employees, it's a good idea to write a title that contains a powerful come-on. Imagine you are giving a talk for a paying audience: what will attract them and persuade them to pay to listen to you? What can they expect to gain from your talk that will help their careers or improve the quality of their lives?

How can you express that benefit in terms that appeal to your target audience? Here's one simple way.

Write down the main strands of your talk, then number them in order of importance. Alongside each add the words, 'which means that ...' and fill in the significance of that point to your audience. Here's an example:

Let's consider a talk on Presentation Skills, provisionally titled 'Improve Your Presentation Skills'. The main strands are:

A. **Why present? Understand that you are not simply transmitting information.** Which means that you will be focused on your objective.

B. **Message. Have something to say.** Which means that you will be relevant, interesting and committed, and offering something new.

C. **Messenger. Really want to say it.** Which means that you will speak with conviction, because the message belongs to you.

D. **Method. Develop the skills to put across your message effectively.** Which means that you probably won't be boring.

E. **Structure.** Which means that you will be prepared and easy to follow.

F. **Visual aids.** Which means that the presentation will be visual as well as auditory.

G. **Know when you are ready.** Which means that you will know when to stop preparing and not overload the content.

H. **Action.** Which means that your listeners will know what to do to take advantage of the techniques you describe.

You can decide for yourself the order of priority in which you would put these strands, if you were giving the talk. For me, the important items are B, C, A, H and D, and I would expect to create my talk title from them.

What's the benefit for listeners that arises out of all those points?
♦ B is about offering something new
♦ C is about commitment to B
♦ A focuses on H
♦ H is the promised action to gain the benefit
♦ D is the means of making it happen.

You could call the talk:

Improve Your Presentation Skills

and that would be legitimate.

Or you could call it something like:
How To Get the Results You Want When You Present

Or you could write a different title. Why not do so now?

The title should make plain what the topic is, and include a major benefit for those within the target audience. There is no need to consider those outside the target group, as that would tend to dilute the strength of the message you could convey.

'How to ...' is always strong, because it signals skills or secrets that are going to be imparted. 'What's new in ...' is another powerful puller for similar reasons. Another good approach is to identify a common fear or problem and promise the antidote. An example of this would be 'Everything you've ever wanted to know about ... but were afraid to ask'.

Match your title to your audience

One word of caution from Roger Alton, Editor of *The Observer*, who says about headlines, 'You have to have your eye on the reader. If you do a headline that is too clever-clever, it irritates them. If you write stuff that isn't immediately comprehensible, you are going to irritate them; if you patronize them, if you make things obscure, you will lose them.'

Having written your title, stand back from it for a moment and ask yourself if it would intrigue or attract you, and whether you would pay to attend such a talk. If you get the title right, it can pre-condition your audience, putting them in the right frame of mind even before you start.

So much for the benefit to the (prospective) audience. What about the benefits to the presenter – yourself? Can the process of writing an enticing title have any serious value to you? It certainly can, and will. As you follow the process described above to identify what your speech or presentation is really about, and what it will offer or provide for your listeners, you will gain a clearer understanding of your purpose. You will realise why you are speaking and what your personal expertise is. You will also become much more aware of your responsibility to your listeners, and that your task is more than to throw words and ideas at them.

Most importantly, the process should help you to identify your **Core Message**, which is the 'take-away benefit'. It's the single sentence that sums up the essence of your entire presentation. It's what you should hope people will remember long after you have finished ... and act upon. It's the CHANGE that you should want to bring about through your talk.

That focus is an essential part of your preparation. Added to the pre-conditioning factor I mentioned above, it underlines the importance of writing the right title for all your talks.

In summary ...

- Your talk's title is a vital part of 'selling' the talk to your audience.
- Highlight the main benefit, not just the content.
- Include the topic as well as the main benefit.
- Think of the title as the headline of an advertisement.
- Appeal to your audience's self interest.
- Be clear and to the point, not clever-clever.
- Writing the title helps to focus your mind on your purpose.

Chapter 4

What's your core message?

In this Chapter:

- **focus, providing benefit for sexy title**
- **how will people summarize your talk when they leave?**
- **understanding how we remember the content of a talk**
- **keeps you on track**
- **don't try to make the definitive statement**
- **identify your contribution to the subject**
- **offer ONE idea that changes people's thinking on the subject.**

Communication is simply the process by which you convey to someone else something that you know or feel, in such a way that the other person understands and receives it, making it part of his or her own fund of knowledge. It is a two-way process. It is not enough simply to transmit. That would be no better than speaking into a telephone without first ensuring that there is someone at the other end of the link.

Acceptance and understanding are essential parts of the process. If the other person does not understand what you are saying, or does not accept it, the communication will fail. The way to avoid such failure is to deliver a message, not just information.

What's your Core Message?

When you have completed your presentation or speech, what will people remember? What will they take away with them, to apply and change their ways, and one day perhaps even thank you for? What one sentence will correctly sum up your entire presentation? That's your **Core Message**.

Make no mistake: your listeners will take away a core message of sorts. They will carry away an impression of what you were saying. It may be complimentary, it may be less so. It may be about you and your delivery, or it may be about your content. If you want them to receive and carry away the right message – *your* Core Message – you must first identify what you believe it to be and write it down.

In the next chapter you will read how the Core Message fits into the process of collecting your content, and how it provides the focus for the ideas you gather. Here, however, let me take you through the reasons why it is so important, and the contribution the Core Message makes to the success of your communication.

How people remember what was said

As the presenter, you have prepared the text, you know what you want to say, you are clear in your own mind as to how each section of your material connects with the section before and the one that follows. You deliver your message at an average speed of perhaps 150 words per minute.

Who, in your audience, is capable of remembering every one of those words? In a 30 minute presentation, you will utter some 4,500 words – far too many for anyone to retain and recall. And it's not just the words: it's the sequence and structure of your arguments that the audience must try to understand and remember. It's a considerable task, so you do need to help them, and a good starting place is to consider what goes on in the minds of an attentive listener.

The listener makes a summary and stores that summary in the memory. For that process to work, the listener needs to know:

◆ what's the point you are trying to make?
◆ where is the evidence?
◆ is it easy to understand?
◆ does it support what you say?

This presupposes that you have a message to impart.
Information on its own is not enough. Indeed, it's much harder to take in and remember yards of information delivered at 150 words per minute. During a poorly

prepared presentation or speech, people in the audience keep asking themselves, 'Where is he/she going with this?' So imagine that your own audience is asking the same question, and make sure you constantly answer it, and satisfy their need to know.

> We sometimes get all the information, but
> we refuse to get the message.
>
> **Cullen Hightower**

You will do best by knowing what your core message is, and focusing your mind on it. Whenever I talk about making speeches or presentations, my core message is **that the main purpose of a speech or presentation is to bring about change**. I make that point early and repeat it whenever appropriate. I focus my talk on that point, so that I drive it home directly and indirectly, showing my listeners how each element of a talk contributes to bringing about the desired change.

What are the guidelines for identifying a Core Message?

The key words are:
◆ relevance
◆ ownership
◆ significance
◆ benefit.

Relevance: Never forget that every member of your audience is tuned into the same radio station: WII FM. What's In It For Me? When considering whether to attend a talk or presentation, people tend to make their decision based on three things:

1 What will be said.
2 Who will be saying it.
3 How is it likely to be said.

In the business context, it is the subject matter that counts most. So your message must be of relevance, significance and interest to your audience, and the title of your speech or presentation must signal that strongly (see Chapter 3). Treat the title as the headline of an advertisement for your talk, putting in the main benefit you are offering. (You *are* offering some benefit, aren't you?)

What will bring your audience to hear you if they do not have to? The subject matter itself will be of interest, or they would not come in the first place. That's a given. But if they had to pay to hear you, and come to your talk instead of going to the theatre or out for a meal, what will inspire them to choose you? And would *you* pay to hear you speak on the subject?

Ownership: There may be some merit in presenting information or ideas that others have developed, but it is far more powerful to offer your own thinking. By that I mean either some original material that you have developed yourself, or your personal spin on someone else's stuff. It is important that the message you impart belongs to you: that it originated within you, that it is something you really want others to know. It doesn't matter if it arose as a reaction to someone else's material, so long as the reaction is your own.

Think of it like this: suppose you are a marketing expert and you are going to speak about **Direct Marketing**. Inevitably you will be telling your audience things they already know. Why should they listen to you instead of reading one of the many excellent books on Direct Marketing? Because they want to hear about *your* experience, and *your* take on the subject. They want to hear:

◆ what *you* think
◆ what you want *them* to think, as well as
◆ anything new you have to offer on the subject.

Another element of their interest is to discover if you can confirm what they already know. Most people don't know how much they know, and they would like an expert (you) to confirm and acknowledge the validity of their existing knowledge, then place it in the context of the whole subject and add the latest developments. It gives them an idea of where they stand in the hierarchy of experts. When asked why they attend seminars and conferences, a high percentage of people will say, 'To find out how much I know'.

It is therefore vital to filter the facts, to tell your audience what you consider to be the meaning of those facts, and how those facts are relevant to your message.

Significance: If your purpose is to bring about change (and it surely must be!), your core message must have the weight to justify such an expectation. It is not enough to label your content and hand it over to your listeners, leaving it to them to decide on its significance. You must do so for them.

A good way to arrive at a significant message is to pick up each strand of your content and ask the question, 'So what?' Imagine a sceptical listener sitting with arms folded, asking that very question. You need to have a convincing answer, and as you deliver that answer you will focus your mind on why it is important for your audience to listen to what you have to say.

Significance is closely related to relevance, and you will understand both when you challenge yourself with sceptical questions. As mentioned above, relevance derives from the question, 'What's in it for me?' When you have answered that question, ask yourself, 'So what?' Then you will know if you have a point of view that might matter to your audience.

How important is it that you speak?

- How will it benefit them?
- What would be the consequence of not going along with you?
- Will it matter if you never gave the speech or presentation?

These are questions that go directly to the heart of the importance of *your* message – not the subject itself, but your take on the subject. Far too many talks are better not given at all. They waste the time of the audience and the time and energy of the speaker. They deliver material that can be better read from books, they offer no new insights, they do nothing to enhance the understanding of their listeners.

Yet, in many instances, that could have been changed very easily, if only the speaker had taken a little trouble to find the answers to the sort of questions I have asked above. The audience is there because the subject matter is relevant to their interests. What they do not know in advance is whether you will be able to add some worthwhile new dimension to their knowledge and understanding. They hope you will, and they will be sorely disappointed if you do not.

On the other hand, there is no need to torture yourself about it. Just look within yourself and ask what you have to offer on the subject that they cannot get from someone else. It may not be information. It is far more likely to be your point of view. So challenge your content. Pick up each factual statement in your text and ask, 'So what?' Ask yourself what you really think about the topic, and why your opinion might be more valid than the opposite one.

Identify what YOU have to say

You will know when you have found the key. As soon as you identify your personal message, and what it is that you want others to know, your spirits will rise. You will feel a surge of energy because you will no longer be afraid of not remembering what to say; you will no longer be anxious about your credentials; you will know that you have something to say, something that comes from within you, and about which you can speak eloquently, because it's what you believe.

I once saw Peter Thomson guide a speaker towards an understanding of his personal core message just by asking him the same simple question several times in a row. Peter had asked him to state what his expertise was, and when the speaker had answered, Peter said, 'Which means that ...?'

The speaker gave his second layer answer, and Peter again said, 'Which means that ... ?' And again and again and again. They must have drilled down through at least six layers until at last the speaker came up with an answer that encapsulated his personal core message. Each time the question was asked, the speaker became a little more uncomfortable, because he was used to giving facile, even superficial, explanations of who he was and what his personal expertise happened to be. Until he went through the exercise with Peter, he had not properly identified who he was and what he could bring to the party whenever he made a speech.

You can, and should, apply the same kind of challenge to your speeches. If you do, it will make a huge difference to the way you feel about giving the speech, and to the way your listeners will respond, because you will have conviction in the way you speak. You will have a purpose, and you will be clear about the message you wish to impart.

That's what will make you a speaker that others will want to hear. A speaker that others will be prepared to pay to hear.

In summary ...

◆ **Identify the single most important idea.**
◆ **Make it simple to understand and remember.**
◆ **Information must be filtered and interpreted.**
◆ **Key words: relevance, ownership, significance, benefit.**
◆ **Know why it's you speaking.**
◆ **Answer the 'so what?' question about your facts.**
◆ **Be clear about your core message and people will want to hear you.**

Chapter 5

Mining your brain for usable content

In this Chapter:

◆ **how to brainstorm**

◆ **do not edit – everything is usable**

◆ **examples of brainstorming**

◆ **number every idea**

◆ **how creativity works**

◆ **what to do when you finally dry up**

◆ **differentiate between fact and opinion**

◆ **what can you substantiate?**

What do you want to talk about?

I was helping a young man prepare a major presentation which he hoped would raise his profile within the company. After the usual preliminaries, I asked him to talk me though his intended message. I said, 'Without trying to make your presentation at this moment, just tell me what you want your audience to know.'

His eyes glazed over and he launched into a rambling discourse that I found hard to follow. He started by saying, 'I don't know what you know about (his subject) ...' and proceeded to tell me all he knew, dwelling on side issues along the way and relishing the kinds of arcane details that technical experts tend to enjoy. From the listener's point of view it was like a treasure hunt in the woods without a map, in which the leader kept changing direction without warning. Clearly he needed help with structure as much as content, but above all he needed focus. He had not thought out what he wanted to say and why. He got stuck in the wrong groove, the one of self-enjoyment, and lost sight of the need to keep his listener (me) with him.

I suggested listing all the ideas he wanted to consider including in his presentation, and asked him to start with a blank page. At the top I asked him to write his **Core Message**. He looked puzzled.

I said, 'Your Core Message is the 'take-away' idea. It's what you want people to remember when they have heard your presentation and leave. It's what they should remember and act on the next day, the next week, and on into the future. The Core Message is the essence of your talk. You need to write it at the top of your page so that you can focus your mind on relevant ideas.'

Persistence pays

I then asked him to draw a line down the middle of the page. My purpose was to discourage him from writing long sentences. All he needed were four or five words on each idea he came up with. Also, in this way he was more likely to get all his ideas on the same page. The guidelines I gave him were:

1   Number all your ideas.
2   No editing: put down every thought, however wild, on your topic.
3   Don't dwell on any one idea. Put it down and move on.
4   No complete sentences: just a few words on each.
5   Keep going even when you think you have dried up.

He quickly listed a dozen items, then more slowly got to 18. He said, 'I think I'll stop at 20' and he wrote the numbers 19 and 20 towards the bottom of the page. Two new ideas came to him and he wrote them alongside those numbers. Then he put down his pen.

I asked him a question and his answer provided item 21. Another question and he had item 22. The next question produced a three-part answer for item 23. We continued until we had 32 items on his list. No prizes for guessing that the last 12 contained some of the best gems. If he had stopped at 20, they would have been missing from his presentation.

That's why I say you must continue even when you think you have dried up. The few extra ideas are often the best.

Be focused

It is important to write your Core Message at the top of the page, to prompt you to produce relevant ideas. However, one word of caution: do not attempt to write the definitive work on your subject, nor an encyclopedia. Your purpose must not be to demonstrate your complete mastery of the subject. It is not about you. It is about the needs of your audience. What you tell your audience in a presentation must be limited to whatever will help you to bring about some change in their thinking, attitude or behaviour.

It is unrealistic to expect that you can turn them into experts in the 30 or 40 minutes that you take to deliver your message. Could you become an expert just by listening to someone speak for that length of time? Obviously not. So limit yourself to whatever is relevant to your message, although you should not reject even the most far-fetched idea, just as long as it is relevant.

Here's an example of 50 brainstormed ideas for a presentation to people who want to be professional speakers. Among the greatest concerns of such people is, 'What should I talk about?' The presentation is therefore about Topic Development, or **How to Make a Speech That People Will Want to Hear.**

CORE MESSAGE: To be a professional speaker you must have something to say and really want to say it, but ensure that it is relevant to the interests of your listeners.

50 IDEAS:

1 Purpose: make change.
2 What change can *you* make?
3 What change(s) do you want to make?
4 What do you believe?
5 What are you good at?
6 What are you expert in?
7 What one thing is identified with you/you with it?
8 What do you want to improve?
9 What do you want people to know? Filter the facts.
10 What can they do with it?
11 What makes you really angry?
12 Ask 'so what?'
13 What qualifies *you*?
14 Ask yourself: who are you? What are your credentials?
15 Defined by physical characteristics/occupation/skills/expertise/belief?
16 Who is your (intended) audience?
17 The audience's expectations?
18 Can you be amusing?
19 Be a meaningful specific, not wandering generality (Ziglar).
20 Walk barefoot in the grass.
21 Never speak on what you don't believe in.
22 Process of persuasion.
23 Tell own stories.
24 Lessons from own experiences.
25 Share your insights.
26 Milton: 'A good teacher is one whose spirit enters the soul of the pupil.'

27 Try out parts of message on friends.

28 What's your core message, i.e. 'take away idea'?

29 What keeps you awake?

30 What keeps them awake?

31 Write your exit line first.

32 Why should they want to listen?

33 What do you get excited about?

34 What makes people listen? what/who/how?

35 Something you know a lot about, audience knows a little.

36 Timely and appropriate.

37 Narrow focus.

38 Able to get response/action.

39 Test by playing devil's advocate.

40 Your preferred epitaph?

41 What outcome do you want at the end?

42 How relevant is the Message?

43 How committed is the Messenger (you)?

44 How good is the Method?

45 Develop signature stories.

46 Create word pictures.

47 Ask rhetorical questions.

48 Don't make a good speech – make a great one!

49 Plan an easy structure plus emotional curve.

50 Is your speech adaptable for different occasions?

The list could go on and on, because some of these ideas suggest others. However, the list is long enough, and there is ample material here on which to base a speech or seminar for budding professional speakers.

Prepare a Hook

The next step is to group the ideas, fitting them to a planned structure and dropping those that do not fit well. In Chapter 8 I shall do just that, and explain the process in greater detail. For now, however, Items 1 and 9 combine well to provide a Hook that is consistent with the Core Message. The Hook is the opening device that grabs attention and leads naturally to the theme of your speech. It should not be merely to startle your audience into paying attention so that you can then jump into your (unconnected) speech. That's a tactic employed by some inexperienced speakers, and all it does is irritate and alienate your audience.

An example would be to stand up and declare: 'Sex!! Now that I have your attention ...' I've heard that done so often that I have resolved to leave the room ostentatiously if I ever hear it done again.

The Hook could be something like this:

Why do you make a speech? Is it to convey information? That's what many people think, but if all you want to do is communicate information, send it by e-mail. Or put it on one side of a small piece of paper and send it to your audience. That's more efficient.

But if you want to make a speech or presentation in person, you need to understand that you have two purposes that are far more important than the mere transmission of information. First, your task is to filter the facts, to tell people what those facts mean, to help them to know what they should think about the facts, and to understand the implication of those facts.

Second, and even more importantly, your purpose should be to bring about change. Change in the thinking, attitude or behaviour of your listeners. And that requires thought and commitment.

How brainstorming works

The way that brainstorming works is through word association. You need to write your core message at the top of the page because that encourages your brain to open the appropriate gate into your imagination. As soon as the gate is open, a number of ideas will quickly present themselves. As you write them down, each will suggest other, related ideas.

Broadly, there will be two levels of ideas that will spring to mind:
◆ headline or category ideas, and
◆ detailed ones.

The first type are the 'folders', while the second type are 'files', and of course files fit within folders. Don't worry about grouping the ideas as they arise. Just be aware of what normally happens, which is that an idea occurs to us, we set it down, and then immediately start to analyze it and decide whether and where it fits. Put that reflex aside for now. Let the ideas come, and let others flow from them.

Association is important. Think of the times when you can't remember the name of someone you met the other day. What do you do to help you recall? You think of the occasion ... where the meeting took place ... who else was there ... who introduced you ... the sound of the voice of the person doing the introduction ... your first impression of the person you met ...

Those are all associations. Trying to remember the name directly often doesn't work, so we need to approach it indirectly, by thinking of the circumstances associated with receiving the person's name. If that doesn't work, it's best to stop trying and think of something else. Suddenly the name appears!

Something similar is at work when we brainstorm. We allow associations to lead us down unexpected paths, and these can bring us to insights that could add considerably to the impact of our message. That's why it is important not to 'edit' or inhibit the free flow of ideas at this stage, even if some of them seem outlandish.

Archimedes is well remembered for discovering the scientific principle of displacement while he was in his bath. He shouted 'Eureka!' and ran naked into the street. Elias Howe spent years trying to develop a sewing machine, but the answer came to him in a dream about spear-wielding tribesmen.

So brainstorming is much more than a listing of the most obvious points of information to include in your talk. It's a technique that allows your brain to open and wander freely among the possibilities. It makes you receptive to flashes of intuition and new angles on the obvious, some of which may derive from the thoughts that may have been incubating in your subconscious ever since you first started thinking about the subject of your talk.

As ideas come to you, ask the basic questions: who, how, why, what, where, when, and so what. Some of them will lead you outward, some (especially the last) will lead you deeper into the point you are making. It may be the most important question of all to ask, because it defines the relevance of the idea to your audience. If you use a quote, add the source. If you make a claim, produce the evidence. Never risk being challenged and not having the facts to prove what you have said. It could destroy your credibility.

How to brainstorm

If you are brainstorming on your own, it is a good idea to do so somewhere quiet, where you can tap into your personal creativity. No phone calls. No interruptions of any kind. Half close your eyes and retreat into your own head, if you can – into a semi trance, emerging only to scribble down each idea as it comes.

If several of you are brainstorming, it's best to appoint one person as the facilitator. Let that person prompt and prod the rest of you, and write down the ideas on a white board or flip chart, so that the rest of you can see them. You can then concentrate on the creative process, remembering that no negative reactions are allowed. No one can dismiss an idea as bad or rubbish. However, the facilitator should decide if an idea is the same as something that has already appeared on the list, and seek agreement that this is so.

As in solo brainstorming, it is important to ensure that there are no outside interruptions to stop the creative flow. If you set a deadline, that creates helpful tension. But do not quit early. As I said at the start of this chapter, you may dry up after a few minutes, but if you persist for a little longer you may gain some real gems.

One more thing: don't waste the work you do here. Write your list as neatly as you can and keep it in a file for future reference. You will not be using all the ideas on this occasion, but some of them might be useful on another occasion, if only to get you started when you next brainstorm a related topic.

In summary ...

- ◆ **Collect your ideas by brainstorming.**
- ◆ **Let the ideas flow, and do not edit at this stage.**
- ◆ **Persist, even after the ideas dry up.**
- ◆ **Recognize the difference between 'headline' ideas and detailed ones.**
- ◆ **Build on word association.**
- ◆ **Group brainstorming should have a facilitator.**
- ◆ **Look for an idea that could provide the 'Hook'.**
- ◆ **Keep the unused ideas for the next time.**

Chapter 6

Simple structures to develop your arguments

In this Chapter:

- **why follow a structure?**
- **PREP: Position/Proposition – Reason – Example – Position/Proposition**
- **Past – Present – Future**
- **Problem – Cause – Solution**
- **AIDA**
- **Tell x 3.**

What is the purpose of having a structure to follow?

Actually there are three purposes:

1   To help you select what to say.
2   To keep you on track.
3   To help your listeners follow you.

What do you suppose causes people to dry up when put on the spot and asked to 'say a few words' in public, with little or no notice? Is it that they have nothing to say? Actually not. Can you think of any occasion when you have broken off from an informal conversation, saying:

'I need to research that topic, and when I have discovered something to say I shall return and contribute to this conversation'?

It never happens. You don't do it, and neither does anyone else, no matter how widely the conversational topics may range. So it is plain that we all have things to say on most topics, even if it's only to express an opinion.

What causes a person to dry up is not knowing how to select from all the information, ideas and opinions that are available in the brain: what to say first, and what to say next.

How structure helps

Having a few simple structures to follow will largely remove that obstacle. The structure interrogates you. It guides your thinking. It helps you choose something appropriate to say at the start, and then it leads you logically to the next point.

Structure keeps you on track. Although it may be frightening when you first stand to speak, once you are into your stride you may drift far and wide and forget the point you set out to make. Or it may be that you start to enjoy the experience so much that you don't want to impose any discipline on yourself. You may lose track of time and spend far too long on 'setting the scene', so that you have to rush some important parts of the message you want to impart.

At a seminar I once attended, I asked a question for clarification when the first overhead was on display. The presenter then spent about 20 per cent of the seminar's entire allocated time on that point and related issues that he and others raised in response to my question. However, he still had another 25 overheads to show and discuss! And why did that happen? Because he hadn't planned a proper structure.

His approach was linear: he started at a certain point, then added material in some sort of sequence until he got to the end. He could have handled it better if he had provided us with a map at the very start, so that he could have briefly answered my question, then shown us where within the planned structure he intended to give it fuller coverage.

Keeping ourselves on track is not always easy. The temptation to drift is always present, and it diminishes our authority if we appear to be a ship without a rudder.

Five simple structures

The structures I shall cover in this chapter can be used to develop individual arguments or they can be used for the entire speech or presentation. They will ensure that you include the essentials, striking a balance between the pros and cons. They will guide your focus and help you decide what to leave out. This will be apparent when, at the end of this book, I take you through the procedure for implementing the lessons of the book and going from blank page to first draft in just fifteen minutes.

PREP

There are two versions of this structure. The letters stand for:

P = Position or Proposition
R = Reason
E = Example
P = Position or Proposition

Here's how the first version works:

◆ This is what I think *(my Position)* on the subject.
◆ This is why *(my Reason)*.
◆ Here's an Example of what I mean.
◆ That's why I think what I do *(my Position)*.

This structure works well when you know what you want to say and are prepared to make an outright commitment to it. Obviously, there will be circumstances when you would prefer to lead more gently into your opinion, and in such cases this would not be the best structure to follow. However, it is a strongly logical format which prompts you to justify and illustrate your point of view.

It is particularly relevant to interviews and Q&A sessions, when you are put on the spot and expected to answer a question with a cogent, definitive statement of your position on some burning topic of the day. Using PREP, you can launch straight into your response, giving yourself an air of purpose as you do so.

Example:

Q: Do you think correct punctuation is either relevant or necessary?

A: (P)   I think it is both relevant and necessary.

(R   The reason why I say so is that correct punctuation helps meaning, while bad punctuation clouds meaning and reveals the writer as only semi-literate. This can create resistance to the substance of what has been written. What's worse is that the young are being encouraged in bad habits through mobile phone text-message conventions, which could inhibit their ability to cope with proper written English when they go out to work.

(E)   Examples abound. There is the familiar greengrocer's misuse of the apostrophe, as in Apple's and Xmas tree's, and in the increasingly common use of 'it's' instead of the proper possessive pronoun, 'its'. The abbreviations in txt msgs R hard 2 avoid.

(P)   I deplore such solecisms, because I think they are taking written English into anarchy. It is also likely that worthwhile candidates for jobs are being rejected because of their poor punctuation, and important messages may sometimes be scorned for the same reason. That's why I believe correct punctuation to be both relevant and necessary.

This is how the second version works:

- ◆ This is what I would like you to do. (Proposition)
- ◆ Here's why. (Reason)
- ◆ Here's how it will benefit you. (Example)
- ◆ That's why I would like you to do it. (Proposition)

Example:

(P) I'd like you to consider implementing a cross-cultural training programme for all managers in your company, and everyone whose job entails talking to existing customers and prospective new ones.

(R) My reason for proposing this is that cross-culture exists right here, within the company, and among those who use your goods and services. We have multi-cultural staff and multi-cultural customers, and we need to understand how they think and operate, so that we can develop productive relationships with them.

(E) For example, staff members from countries such as France and the Far East may not respond as you'd expect to performance-related pay, and certain Far-Eastern customers may prefer to deal with someone with grey hair, rather than with a young person, however bright and capable that person may be.

(P) By improving the way we connect and communicate with our people within the firm and our customers outside it, we can develop lasting relationships that will improve the company's reputation as well as its trading performance. That's why I propose a cross-cultural training programme as a matter of urgency.

Past, Present, Future

This is one of the easiest structures to follow. It is sometimes called the 'chronological sequence', and it can be applied to develop an individual argument, or it can be the structure of the entire presentation. Here's how it works:

◆ PAST: This is how things used to be.
◆ PRESENT: This is how they are at the moment.
◆ FUTURE: This is how they could/should be.

You can, of course, dress it up a little, as in this example:

◆ Let me first consider the historical background, and see how it has led to our present position.
◆ Let me now turn to the current situation and see what needs to change.
◆ Going forward, the options available to us are ... and the one I believe we should implement is ...

A variation on this structure is to follow the chronology of an event or major development, as in this example:

1 The British monarchy started to change with the abdication of Edward VIII in 1936. The constitutional and political implications were ...
2 Then came the Second World War, and that changed the perceptions and expectations of the British people, so that ...
3 There were the years of austerity, during the 50s, when suddenly there was a new, young Queen on the throne ...

4 The next decade, the so-called Swinging Sixties, brought a major shift in values and attitudes, which resulted in the death of deference, and that carried through to the way in which the nation regarded the royal family ...

5 In the 90s, there were several significant shifts prompted by individual members of the royal family, from the late Princess Diana to ...

Problem, Cause, Solution

This is a structure that lends itself well to business situations and to preparing reports. It says:

◆ This is what is wrong.
◆ Here's what caused it.
◆ This is what we should do about it.

It is, of course, very similar to Past, Present, Future, just in a different order. The Problem is the Present, the Cause is the Past and the Solution is the Future. It can also be used as the structure for the entire Body of your Presentation. Clearly, you can spend a significant amount of time analyzing and explaining the Problem, and an equal amount of time exploring the cause(s) before presenting your proposals for corrective action.

It is very important, in using any chronological structure such as Problem, Cause, Solution and Past, Present, Future to let your audience know when you have finished with each section and are about to address the next one.

If you don't, and if you progress seamlessly from the Past to the Present, some of your listeners will suddenly stop listening as they say to themselves, 'Oh, have we finished with the Past? I wonder how he did that, and what the connection is with the current situation.'

While they are working that out they are not listening to you, and they then have to play catch up ... if they can be bothered. Transitions, or signposts, as they are sometimes called, are always important in every speech or presentation, but especially in chronological structures such as these.

AIDA: Attention, Interest, Desire, Action

Your presentation should be to bring your listeners to your point of view, even if you perceive it as transmitting information. Why would you be transmitting information unless it was new, and you wanted them to do something with the information. That implies persuasion, and the AIDA structure helps you to achieve that. It helps you to raise the interest level of your listeners up to and beyond the 'buying level' – the point at which they are ready to accept your proposition.

A is for Attention. Before you can persuade anyone you must first grab their attention. Your opening should therefore identify your target audience and say, in effect, 'Hey you! Stop! This is for you!'. The right attention-getter will raise interest sharply, but usually not enough to go past the 'buying level', so you have more to do.

I is for Interest, which you build up by piling up the benefits of your proposition. Facts are not enough. They need to be interpreted, and their benefits explained. Don't expect your listeners to work out for themselves the benefits of the points you are making. Do the interpretation for them. When you make an assertion or proposition, go on to add, 'Which means that ...'

Remember that your listeners either have never heard your point of view before, or they are already committed to some alternative viewpoint or way of doing things, which you are seeking to overcome. If you were selling a product, you would be seeking to persuade them to exchange their money for your product. They will not be prepared to make the exchange until your pile of benefits outweighs their pile of money.

D is for Desire. That is the point at which your listeners think, 'I want that!'. It is a point well past the 'buying level', and has to be, because sooner or later you have to tell them what it will cost them to obtain the benefits of your proposition. It doesn't have to be a cash cost: there is an inertia cost as well: 'I've always done things this way, why should I change?' But if you pile the benefits sufficiently high, they will decide that what they gain from your way is worth more than the discomfort of switching from the old way.

A is for Action. Once you have raised your listener's interest to the point of Desire, you must make it easy for them to obtain what you have been offering. This is called 'Closing the Sale', and you should remember that your listeners *expect* you to close the sale. They want you to want their commitment or their business. And they want you to make it easy.

Tell x 3

This is the well-known sequence that goes:

1 Tell 'em what you're going to tell 'em.
2 Tell 'em.
3 Tell 'em what you've told 'em.

You start with an agenda or outline of what you are going to say.
Then you flesh it out.
Finally, you summarize.

Clearly, this could be the structure of your entire presentation. It could be stand-alone or it could be combined with one of the other structures. For example, you could use it together with Past, Present, Future, like this:

Tell 1: I shall cover this subject by first considering the historical perspective *(=Past)*, then examine what is wrong with the current position *(=Present)*, before proposing the changes I believe we should make *(=Future)*.

Tell 2: First, let's see how things used to be, and how they led to the problems we are currently facing. *(Discuss the Past at length, showing the underlying trends.)* Now let's turn to the situation we are in today. What is causing us problems? *(Discuss the Present at length, showing how it is* *connected to the Past.)* Having seen how the past trends have contributed to our current poor performance, we need to break the chain and do things very differently. The options available to us are ... and I propose that we do ... *(Develop the Future at length, proving the value of breaking with historical trends.)*

Tell 3: To summarize, we have seen how the trends that were established in the early days have carried forward to the present time. They are largely responsible for the practices that are stopping us from growing. We need to change, and that's why I propose Option B of the three that are available to us.

In summary ...

- **Structure keeps you on track.**
- **It helps you to select what you should be saying.**
- **It maintains discipline and helps you avoid an imbalance in your content.**
- **These recommended structures can apply to individual arguments or to the whole presentation:**
  PREP
  Past, Present, Future
  Problem, Cause, Solution
  AIDA
  Tell x 3.

Chapter 7

Fit your content to the structure

In this Chapter:

- **place brainstormed ideas alongside template**
- **write numbers in appropriate places**
- **example of how it's done**
- **this is when to edit – discard what does not fit**
- **group all selected ideas into 3 main strands (Body)**
- **identify what can be used as the Hook**
- **the kind of questions to ask yourself.**

The previous chapter gave you several simple structures to help you develop individual arguments. They could also be the structure of the main presentation or speech. For example, you may decide to make your case based on Past / Present / Future: This is how things used to be / Here's where we are at the moment / These are the options available to us for the future. You can deal with each section briefly or at length, according to the occasion and the time you have to speak.

First, however, you need to establish a template for your speech or presentation, into which you will place the points you have brainstormed. I shall show you the template four times, building it from the skeleton to the speaker's notes. At each stage we shall add something new to the template, so that you can see the step-by-step process of creating a workable speech from a list of ideas related to your topic, which you brainstormed earlier.

Taking a step back to the very beginning, the process I have been taking you through may be summed up like this:

♦ Decide on your topic.
♦ Identify your core message.
♦ Brainstorm ideas.
♦ Create a template.
♦ Fit ideas to the template.
♦ Draft your first outline.

Creating your template

How many parts are there to a presentation? That's right – there are three. You probably call them Beginning, Middle and End. Let's re-name them **A, B, C,** partly because that's easier to remember and partly because the new names I'm going to give them are more accurate descriptions of what they are.

♦ **A = Approach**
♦ **B = Body**
♦ **C = Conclusion**

A is for Approach because at the start of your presentation you need to set the scene and indicate, through your Agenda, how you propose to cover your topic. It also signifies your personal style, to how you will be relating to your audience, and to your personal authority.

It contains two elements, both of which are vital in ensuring that you capture the attention of your audience:
◆ The **Hook** and
◆ the **Map**.

The Hook says, 'Stop! This is for you!' while the Map tells them what you will be talking about, and in which order. Both are essential. The Hook is the device for breaking through their indifference or inattention, while the Map is the Agenda, enabling your listeners to identify with you and your topic even before you start to speak.

B is for the Body of your presentation. This is where you will deliver the meat of your talk, developing the facts and the arguments, making your case for the change you want to bring about through your talk. Ideally it should have three strands of argument. If, for example, you were following a Past / Present / Future structure, those headings would represent your three strands of argument.

Why three? Because two are not enough and four are too many. You may want to make 20 points in your talk, but you need to group them into three. There's magic in threes. Three things are easier to remember than four, and you should be structuring your talk to make it easy:

- for you to remember what to say and in what order
- for your audience to understand and follow
- for your audience to remember and make change.

When you make a speech or presentation, you have a limited amount of time in which to get your message across, and your communication process must be highly effective. You therefore need to use all the tools available to connect with your listeners. The **Rule of Three** is already embedded in most people's minds, and therefore provides a ready-made pattern for you to match.

Here are a few well-known groups of three that we commonly use:

- Beginning / Middle / End
- Breakfast / Lunch / Dinner
- Left / Right / Centre
- Morning / Noon / Night
- Top / Middle / Bottom
- Past / Present / Future
- Problem / Cause / Solution
- Win / Lose / Draw
- As easy as A, B, C.

C is for Conclusion. Clearly, you must bring your talk to a close with a bang, instead of just running out of steam and limply saying, 'Thank you'. Moreover, if you have an objective to start with, you need to focus on that at the end, and also let your audience know that you have finished. All that may sound obvious, but in reality a high proportion of presentations simply fizzle out at the end, with an embarrassed pause before the polite applause begins. Don't let it happen to you. A long pause at the end of your presentation, followed by polite but unconvincing applause, will leave you feeling very uncomfortable, with a sense of failure.

There are two elements that form the Conclusion:

◆ a **Summary**
◆ a call to **Action**, or an **Outcome**.

As detailed in the previous chapter, the Summary is a reminder of what you have told your listeners (possibly using different words) – Tell 3 – in which you have the chance to clarify the points you have made. Finally you should tell them what they should do to adopt the new thinking you were urging on them. How can they benefit? How should they respond? What's the next step? What would *you* want to know if you were in their shoes?

Making your template

1. Framework

First, let's use the linear approach, then I'll show you how to mind map your template. Start with a blank page. About one fifth of the way from the top of the page, draw a line across the page. Do the same one fifth of the page up from the bottom. Next, label each of the three sections:

```
A. Approach



B. Body



C. Conclusion


```

Now add the sub-sections, like this:

```
A. Approach
- Hook:
- Map:


B. Body
1. (Strand 1):
2. (Strand 2):
3. (Strand 3):


C. Conclusion
- Summary:
- Action:


```

2. Allocating ideas from your list

Now place your brainstormed ideas (see Chapter 5) alongside the template, and decide which ideas you are going to use, and where. Just write their numbers in the appropriate places on the template – that's why I asked you to number the ideas when you brainstormed them. This is when you can drop any idea that does not fit.

You must bear in mind your **core message** and the **outcome** you want to produce at the end of your talk. The ideas you select must convey that message and lead to the planned outcome. Everything else is irrelevant.

Your page might now look like the one shown below:

TITLE: How to Make a Speech That People Will Want to Hear.

A. Approach

- Hook: 1, 2, 48

- Map: Messenger / Message / Method

B. Body

1. Messenger: 4, 5, 6, 7, 8, 9, 13, 14, 23, 24

2. Message: 3, 10, 11, 17, 28, 29, 30, 41

3. Method: 12, 16, 18, 22, 31, 45, 46, 47, 49, 50

C. Conclusion

- Summary:

- Action: 28, 38, 41

---

3. Extending the numbered ideas

Clearly you will not be using all the points indicated on the template, even though some have already been dropped because they do not add significantly to the content. You may also decide to add new points which did not occur to you when you were first brainstorming, but which arise as you put your selected ideas in place.

They may not be entirely new ideas, but simply different ways of expressing the same thing. Don't be a slave to first thoughts – you are in charge, and you can use new ideas if you think they work better.

The template may now look like this:

TITLE:
How to Make a Speech That People Will Want to Hear.

HOOK:
Why make a speech?
◆ Create change – relevant and beneficial to listeners.
◆ Filter the facts – say what *you* think.
◆ Not a good speech, but a *great* one.
(transition)

AGENDA:
Message: Have something to say.
Messenger: Really want to say it.
Method: Develop appropriate skills.
(transition)

B. BODY

MESSENGER:
- What do you believe?
- What are you good at?
- What are you expert in?
- What one thing is identified with you/you with it?
- What do you want to improve?
- What do you want people to know? Filter the facts.
- What qualifies *you*?
- Ask yourself: who are you? What are your credentials?
- Tell own stories (signature).
- Lessons from own experiences.

(transition)

MESSAGE:
- What change(s) do you want to make?
- What makes you really angry?
- What keeps you awake?
- The audience's expectations?
- What keeps them awake?
- What's your core message, i.e. 'take away idea'?
- What can they do with it?
- What outcome do you want at the end?

You may want to add:
- Do you have something to say?
- How is it relevant/helpful to me?
- Does it belong to you?
- Do you feel passionately about it?
- Can you talk about it at a moment's notice and without notes?

◆ Are you an expert on the subject?
◆ Do you have your own slant on it?

METHOD:
◆ Who is your (intended) audience? (Focus).
◆ Write your exit line first.
◆ Develop signature stories.
◆ Create word pictures.
◆ Ask rhetorical questions.
◆ Ask 'so what?'
◆ Process of persuasion.
◆ Can you be amusing?
◆ Plan an easy structure plus emotional curve.
◆ Is your speech adaptable for different occasions?

You might want to add:
◆ Structure.
◆ Hook: something unusual but relevant.
◆ Precise language.
◆ Make word pictures.
◆ Voice: resonant, pleasant, varied.
◆ Meaningful eye contact.
◆ Movement and gestures conveying sincerity.
◆ Deliver meaning of words, not the words alone.

At this stage all you have done is to assemble the material you may wish to include in your speech. Clearly, you now have more than you might need, and the next step is to select and shape as you write your outline.

4. Creating speaker's notes
(= Your first draft of the speech)

Let's produce the outline as speaker's notes first, following the usual linear format, then do it as a mind map.

LINEAR OUTLINE (Speech Notes)

TITLE:
(Intro)
Going to talk about:
How to Make a Speech That People Will Want to Hear.

A. APPROACH

HOOK:
Challenge: Why make a speech?
◆ Create change – relevant and beneficial to listeners.
◆ Filter the facts – say what *you* think.
◆ Not a good speech, but a *great* one.

(transition) Let's consider the 3 main factors in speech-making.

AGENDA:
Message: Have something to say.
Messenger: Really want to say it.
Method: Develop appropriate skills.

(transition) Let's start with *you* – the Messenger.

B. BODY – (Why, What, How)

MESSENGER – Why

Why you and why this topic
- ◆ Credentials: leading expert.
- ◆ Identified with subject.
- ◆ Signature story.
- ◆ Elevator speech.
- ◆ Lessons from own experiences.

(transition) Now consider relevant Message.

MESSAGE – What

Having something to say
- ◆ What change(s) do you want to make?
- ◆ What makes you really angry?
- ◆ What keeps you awake?
- ◆ What's your core message, i.e. 'take away idea'?

(transition) Message must relate to audience.

Relevant to audience
- ◆ The audience's expectations?
- ◆ What keeps them awake?
- ◆ What can they do with it?
- ◆ What outcome do you want at the end?

(transition) Must come from within you.

Relevant to you
- Does it belong to you?
- Do you feel passionately about it?
- Can you talk about it at a moment's notice and without notes?
- Are you an expert on the subject?
- Do you have your own slant on it?

(transition) Message OK, Messenger OK, what about technique?

METHOD – How

First, the focus
- Who is your (intended) audience?
- Personal? Signature stories
- Adaptable for different occasions?

Next the text
- Structure.
- Hook: something unusual but relevant.
- Precise language.
- Make word pictures.
- Rhetorical questions.
- Write exit line first.

Delivery
- Voice: resonant, pleasant, varied.
- Meaningful eye contact.
- Movement and gestures conveying sincerity.
- Deliver meaning of words, not words alone.

C. CONCLUSION

Summary
- ◆ Have something to say.
- ◆ Really want to say it.
- ◆ Develop professional skills.
- ◆ Focus on audience needs/interests.

Outcome
- ◆ Start with the end in view.
- ◆ Aim to make change, or don't make the speech.
- ◆ If it's a speech worth making, it's a speech worth hearing.

MIND MAPPING

This is not going to be a detailed description of the process and rationale of mind mapping. Rather, it is a simple explanation of how to set out the above speech outline as a mind map or spider diagram.

Mind mapping can be used to help you brainstorm, and it can replace any or all of the four linear stages shown above. However, I shall assume that you follow the listing procedure given in Chapter 5, and use the mind map simply to create order and replace the speaker's notes.

A mind map gives an overview as well as prompting new thoughts, and is a very handy tool for constructing your argument, keeping on track, and speaking from a single sheet of paper.

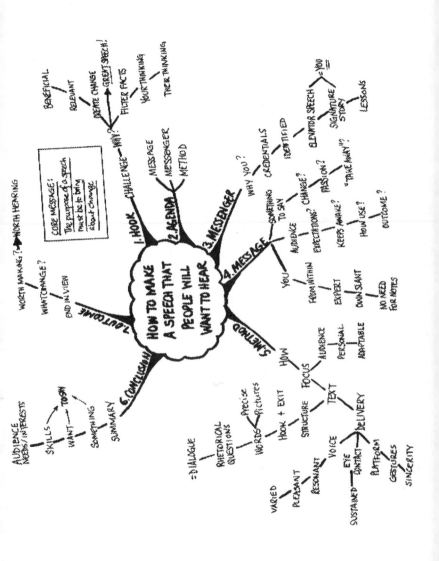

1   Start with a sheet of A4 paper, set sideways (landscape).
2   Write your title in the centre of the page and draw a cloud around it.
3   At the one o'clock position print the word HOOK in capitals.
4   Draw an extended arrowhead under the word, starting at the edge of the cloud and extending outwards.
5   Moving clockwise, add the main headings.
6   Add the related points in descending order, like the branches of a tree, linking them with different coloured lines.

In summary ...

◆ **Create a template for your speech.**
◆ **Base it on Approach / Body / Conclusion.**
◆ **Have three strands of argument in the Body.**
◆ **Allocate ideas from your brainstorming to each part of the template.**
◆ **Write your outline as headings and bullets.**
◆ **Alternatively, make a mind map from the brainstormed ideas.**
◆ **Add new ideas as they occur during this process.**
◆ **Do not lose sight of your core message.**

Chapter 8

First Draft Speech from Speaker's Notes

'How to make a speech that people will want to hear'

This is the speech that could be given from the Speaker's Notes created in the previous chapter, to demonstrate the viability of such an outline, which you could produce from scratch in just fifteen minutes.

OPENING:

Ladies and gentlemen.

As the Chairman has told you, I am here to talk about how you can make a speech that others will want to hear. So let me say right away that I shall not be talking about how you can make a *good* speech. No, I want to talk about how you can make a *great* speech. And to do that I need to clarify one or two fundamental points of understanding between us.

HOOK:

Let me ask you this: why do you make a speech? What is your purpose? *(Wait for answers.)*

Whenever I ask that question, someone will say that it is to communicate information. They may use different words, but that is the most common answer. Indeed, that is the most common misapprehension about the purpose of a speech. Because, if you want to communicate information, my advice is to put it on one side of a small piece of paper and mail it to your audience, or else send them an e-mail. It's far more efficient that way.

No, your purpose in making a speech is not to communicate information, but to bring about change: change in the thinking, attitude or behaviour of your audience. And when you give them information, you must filter the facts. You must tell them what you think about those facts and what you want them to think about those facts. And even more importantly, what you want them to *DO* with those facts.

You see, information on its own is neutral. It means very little unless you give it a context, and compare it with something else. For example, you might say that your company's profits went up by 10 per cent last year. But is that good? If all your competitors made a loss in the same period, it's terrific news. But if they all increased their profits by an average of 25 per cent, your 10 per cent figure is not very good news.

Equally, you could say that your company performed better than its competitors by a large margin. But so what?

If your audience is your staff, they will want to know how that will be of benefit to them. Will they share in the increased earnings? Will there be a larger Christmas bonus this year? What's the point of telling them of the increased profits? That's what will be in their minds.

And if your audience consists of market analysts from the stock exchange, you will want them to recommend your company's shares and tell the market what a bargain they are at the current level.

You see, it all depends on the context that you give the information. It depends on the filter that you place upon the information. That's what makes the information either interesting or just humdrum, and that's what makes you such an important part of the communication process when you make a speech.

(transition:) So let's consider the three most important factors in speech making.

AGENDA:

They are the Message, the Messenger and the Method. The Three Ms.

What that means is that, if you want to speak in a way that makes others want to listen,
- You must have something to say.
- You must really want to say it.
- You must have the technique for putting it across effectively.

The way I shall tackle it is by matching those three elements to three fundamental questions: Why, What and How.

The **Why** relates to you: why is it you speaking and why this topic.
The **What** relates to the topic and what you have to say about it.
The **How** relates to the way you put it together and how you put it across.

(transition) Let's start with *you* – the Messenger. Let's consider why it's you speaking and why it is this topic.

B. BODY – (Why, What, How)

MESSENGER – Why

There are three reasons why people would choose to attend a talk, especially if they had to pay their own money to attend. Those three reasons are:

- ◆ What's being said?
- ◆ Who is saying it?
- ◆ How will it be said?

Those three reasons exactly match the Three Ms:
- ◆ What's being said is the Message.
- ◆ Who is saying it is about the Messenger.
- ◆ And How it will be said is about the technique of the speaker.

It is therefore essential to establish your credentials. What makes you an expert? What entitles people to expect knowledge, wisdom or something new from you? When they think of this subject, do they also think of you? And when they think of you in the round, do they also think of this subject as being part of your claim to fame?

Are you and this subject inextricably linked?

If you had to give your elevator speech, would it include some reference to this subject? For those who do not know what an elevator speech is, it is a fifteen second statement of who you are and what you do, expressed in such a way as to prompt people to ask for more. It focuses your mind on your own particular expertise and the benefit you can offer.

It's called an Elevator Speech because you should imagine getting into an elevator or a lift and being asked by stranger: 'What do you do?' You have between that floor and the next (say fifteen seconds) to give an answer that offers some benefit to anyone who might be in the market for your services.

Why you and why this topic

Of course, being an expert is not enough. What matters even more is how and why your topic should be of interest to your audience.

Here's when you must take a hard, objective look at why you are making the speech. If it is to flatter your ego, don't make the speech. If it is to tell them something that they could just as easily read for themselves, don't make the speech. If it is in any way out of duty rather than conviction, don't make the speech.

Only make the speech because you have something to say, something that adds to your listeners' understanding of the topic, something that matters deeply to you and which also can benefit your listeners. Make it personal to you and illustrate it with an anecdote or two from your own experience. And tell them what you learned from the experience.

Let's consider what might be a relevant message for your speech.

MESSAGE – What

Having something to say

Having something to say means more than just having an interesting idea. It's much more. It's about an idea that is burning within you, keeping you awake at night, arousing strong passions in you. It may be something that makes you really angry. It may be something that has got you in a state of high excitement. It may be a new discovery or a new way of looking at things.

Whatever it is, it's something that you are dying to share with others, to change their thinking, or their attitudes or their actions. When you have an idea that moves you so strongly, it's a message worth hearing.

But that is only half the battle won.

(transition) Your Message must relate to your audience and their interests.

Relevant to audience

You must relate it to their needs and show how it can help them achieve what is important to them. It may keep you up at night, but will it keep them awake? You need to express your idea in a sentence or two, to form your core message or 'take away' idea. But express it in a way that relates to your audience.

Ask yourself these questions:

◆ What are their expectations?
◆ What are the anxieties that keep them awake at night?
◆ How does your idea relate to those anxieties or needs?

And when you have the answers to those questions, remind yourself to focus on the outcome that you want. In other words, what do you want your listeners to do with your core message?

(transition) In fact, this would be a good time to consider how the core message relates to you. Above all, it must come from within you.

Relevant to you

- Does it belong to you?
- Do you feel passionately about it?
- And can you talk about it at a moment's notice and without notes?

An audience can sense if your speech is simply a rehash of someone else's thinking. The material may not be new, but the thinking, the filter, the point of view, that must belong to you. And if it does, you will not need notes to speak from, except to help keep you on track. You will usually need notes to remind you of factual content, but you should not need notes to remind you of what you *think* about those facts.

You are the world's greatest expert on your own point of view, as long as you have thought about the topic and have your own slant on it. That's when you can think of yourself as an expert with something to say that is worth hearing.

(transition) All right, we've considered how we can ensure that the Message is OK, and the Messenger is OK, but what about technique? How do we put our thoughts together and put them across in a way that makes others want to listen?

METHOD – How

First, the focus

First, find your focus. Find out all you can about your audience, and write down their characteristics and what you think they will want to hear.

Develop **signature stories** that are about you, but which you can adapt to suit each type of audience. You can take a fairy story and add a personal twist to make it relevant to your point of view. You can make up a fable and do the same thing.

People love hearing stories, and if there is a lesson to be learned from them, that's even better. Stories remind us of our childhood, and they are easy to relate to. We can all place ourselves within the story and experience the reactions that lead to the moral or lesson that is drawn at the end.

So stories are good. They are also good because they enable your listeners to make pictures in their minds, and that will help them to understand you better.

Next the text

Something else that will help them to stay on track with you is a visible **structure**. For example, if you tell them that you are going to talk about the past, then the present situation, before considering the future, they will know what to expect, and where they are along the way.

Never forget to use a **Hook** at the start. You always need something to grab the attention of your audience and focus their minds. Your Hook needs to be something unusual or unexpected, but relevant to your topic.

Just as important is your **exit line**. Your Hook gets you off to a good start, but your exit line launches your core message into the future. It's what your listeners have the best chance of remembering, because it comes at the very end. So plan both at the same time.

Use precise language that can be easily understood, and avoid terms that can be misheard. One of my dearest friends wanted to make an important speech in which she would refer to Britain as a 'Second Ray' country, using an analogy drawn from her philosophical readings.

After she had used the term two or three times, I realised that she was not calling Britain a 'second rate' country. I suggested that she might say Britain was a country of 'The Second Ray'. Similarly, if you speak quickly and swallow the opening syllables of negative words like, 'inconsiderate', you could convey the opposite impression to what you intend. Better to use stand-alone positive versions, such as 'selfish'.

One very useful device for involving your audience in an unspoken dialogue is the **'rhetorical question'**. A rhetorical question does not require an answer, either because the answer is obvious, or because you are about to provide the answer in the very next breath.

However, the rhetorical question is the question in the minds of your listeners. It is their question, so they feel involved. And example would be. 'So what's next?' And your listeners will be thinking, 'Yes, what *is* next?'

Delivery

And speaking of rhetorical devices, what about **Delivery**? Is it important to use your voice and other platform mechanics to make more of your message? It certainly is.

You see, a speech is much more than mere amplified conversation. It's a performance. It therefore demands performing skills. Your voice should be resonant, pleasant and varied.

Your **eye contact** needs to embrace every member of the audience. Not superficially, not for a mere half second at a time, but for three to five seconds from time to time.

Your movement and gestures should be meaningful and sincere, and you should aim to deliver the meaning of the words, not the words alone. Talk *to* your audience, not *at* them.

C. CONCLUSION

Summary

Finally, let me sum up. If you want to speak in a way that makes others want to listen, you must have something to say, and you must really want to say it. Always express it in terms that relate to the interests of your listeners, and develop professional skills, both in the preparation and in the delivery of your speech.

Outcome

Always start with the end in view.

Aim to make change, or don't make the speech.

If it's a speech worth making, it's likely to be a speech worth hearing. And that's the challenge.

Chapter 9

When you need to be succinct

In this Chapter:

- ◆ **why you should get to the point**
- ◆ **13 situations when it pays to prepare**
- ◆ **how good communication skills are part of leadership**
- ◆ **how you can save expensive executive time**
- ◆ **speaking at a moment's notice**
- ◆ **making a better impression in job interviews**
- ◆ **making a greater impact in meetings.**

When you need succinct communication

There are far more situations than you might imagine when it is important to present your case clearly and succinctly. As explained in Chapter 1, you should never consider busking it, even if you have only a few minutes to prepare. Always make the time. As the rest of this book demonstrates, once you have the technique, all you need is fifteen minutes to produce a workable outline. The effect on your outcome will be considerable.

It is not only desirable to plan every presentation, it is *essential*. This chapter will provide a simple guide to the kind of thinking that should precede every presentation, both formal and informal, but first let's consider the many situations in which it will pay to prepare.

Pitching for new business

This is the most obvious situation in which you need to prepare a structured presentation that connects with the prospect's needs while emphasising the benefits that you can offer. Overlook one important ingredient, or follow the wrong sequence, and your impressive credentials may count for nothing.

One very useful exercise is to prepare the presentation with all the visual aids you need, and then to pretend you have been given only two minutes or five or some other small number of minutes, and have to present in that time and without any visual aids. Try it and you will be amazed at how it focuses your mind on your core message, and forces you to follow a structure.

You will need to ask yourself: what do they *need* to know to make a decision, and what do I *need* to tell them to ensure that they decide in my favour.

Presenting creative work

If you are a writer, your word skills will be under scrutiny when you present. It's no consolation to plead that your skill is with the written word rather than the spoken word, if your presentation is rambling and your listeners switch off, dismissing your work because you did not put your point across impressively.

The questions to ask yourself are: what's the thrust of my work? Why have I chosen to express it in *this* way? Remember that most people have their own ideas on copy and design, and it is a rare discussion on a creative approach that does not include suggestions for changing what you first proposed. You may have slaved for three days over a piece of work, yet someone else will pick up a pen and expect to improve it *immediately!* But if you have prepared a concise rationale for your approach, you will startle them into acceptance.

Asking for a rise

This is a selling situation in which many people find themselves, even if they do not think of themselves as having selling skills. It's a situation in which you must persuade your boss to give you something that matters to you, and which he or she had not already decided to give you. It requires the preparation of a well-reasoned case that presses the right buttons in the right order.

This is one situation when you can expect that your listener does not start out in a receptive frame of mind. In fact, he or she (i.e. your boss) almost certainly does not want to hear your message, because it is usually outside the planned programme of annual rises. You will therefore be faced with a low level of tolerance, and must get to the point quickly, but in a controlled manner, so that you can still make your persuasive case and gain acceptance of your arguments.

Leading a team

Clear communication skills is one of the most significant factors in leadership. If you can articulate what others are struggling to say, and if you can demonstrate a structured approach to achieving your group objectives, others will follow you. The easiest decision for others to take is to follow the one who knows or seems to know. If you have the ability to express what others are trying to crystallize in their minds, they are likely to stop trying to do it themselves and simply go along with what you say. (See Brainstorming below.)

In any group, the one who consistently expresses a cogent argument in a well-structured way is the one who gets noticed and the most airtime. That could be you, especially if you follow the disciplines given in this book, and *PRACTISE*.

Brainstorming

Pooling ideas can be a highly effective way of starting to solve a problem or present a proposition. But it can also be a waste of time. It all depends on the structure and discipline within which the brainstorming is carried out. On one occasion I was part of a team that was brought together to pool ideas for a new business pitch. From 9:30am until 12 noon the conversation rambled all over the place, getting nowhere. In frustration, I asked to take over and in half an hour of structured brainstorming we arrived at a mind map for the entire proposal document!

On another occasion, I was asked to lead a meeting to compose the basis for a major presentation to the entire staff of a large insurance company. The seven top directors present had a tendency to thrash out every point that arose, and we could have been there all day. I proposed a sequence and structure and asked them simply to flesh out the points in my structure, and in one hour we had completed the task, with a workable outline.

The beauty of brainstorming is its unpredictability. Sometimes the least likely idea can develop into the fresh approach that were seeking. It is vital that the creative process in brainstorming is given its head and not inhibited by form or preconceptions. You can brainstorm straight on to a mind map, or you can first make a list, then fit the selected points on to a mind map which forms the first outline of your speech. (See Chapter 8.)

Mind mapping and brainstorming go together. They mirror the way the mind works. Think of a subject and your mind immediately flashes up several ideas or lines of attack. You can follow any one of them and they lead to related points and sub points, just like the branches of a tree, extending all the way out to the tiniest twigs. It's up to you to decide how deep to go. When you have finished, the mind map gives you an overview as well as the complete outline on a single page.

Chairing a meeting

It's amazing how in many meetings the chairperson busks it, as though they need less preparation than the speakers. A good chairperson, on the other hand, prepares an opening statement that sets out the ground rules, establishes the theme and creates the right environment for the speakers to flourish and give of their best. That requires thought and preparation ... and structure.

The Chairperson should have the ability to summarize a speech in a few words, and pick out the points that may need expanding, perhaps also re-structuring the main points to help everyone to understand and retain the message of the speech.

Making a speech

Like new business presentations, a speech is a persuasive activity. Your purpose is (and should be) to bring about some change in the thinking, attitude or behaviour of your listeners. It is not enough to string together some unconnected jokes and anecdotes. On the other hand, it can be a terrifying prospect if called upon, at short notice, to deliver a speech. As I have already mentioned, this book came about because my friend Sylvia Milton once saw the way I coped with making a speech with only 10 minutes' notice. She said, 'Why not analyze how you did that, and teach others to do so as well.'

There are certain occasions when it is desirable to learn a speech by heart, but most of the time a speech will ring true if the words are improvised around a prepared structure. The process described in this book is based on the use of content that is already in your head. It shows you how to select the material or ideas you should be using, and how to organize it. If you know the subject matter you should be able to talk about it without being slave to a written text.

Seminars

Seminars are educational or instructional sessions conducted by experts, to small groups of advanced students or others who know the subject rather well. Seminars imply the exchange of ideas, and there is always the temptation to stray far and wide, unless the seminar leader has a clear vision and well-defined structure for the session.

Training sessions

Ever found yourself underprepared for a training session and decided to trot out the same old same old? Stop! If you know your stuff you can quickly put together a new agenda, one which will excite you and therefore sound so much more interesting to others. Use the disciplines in this book to give yourself and your training a fresh focus.

Job interviews

There is a temptation to regard job interviews as reactions to questions. You've sent in your CV and now you are waiting to answer any questions that may be put to you. However, you can and should prepare. Focus on the message and impression you want to convey. You will then be able to influence the direction of the interview. Anticipate typical questions such as, 'Why do you want this job?' and prepare a short but engaging reply that trips off the tongue!

Selling a product or service

Salesmen who start a selling interview without proper preparation are merely inflicting their personalities on their prospects. It will not do. It is discourteous to the person who has agreed to give time and attention, and it is waste of an opportunity to do business. Whether the sales presentation is to one person or to a large audience, the thought processes are pretty much the same.

Reporting to the Board

Board meetings tend to be about strategy, and when you are asked to present a report to the board, you will be expected to be brief and to the point, avoiding nitty gritty detail. You will also be expected to cover the ground in terms that they can all understand. Your subject may be technical, but your audience will almost certainly not be.

Campaign briefing

Whether you are briefing a creative team on a mailing or an advertising campaign, or an agency for a piece of research, they will want a structured approach that tells them clearly what your objective is and what you want them to include. Remember that what you say is not always what others receive, and your communication needs to be clear and concise if you want to get the best result.

In summary ...

It helps to be brief and to the point in:

- ◆ pitching for new business
- ◆ presenting creative work
- ◆ asking for a rise
- ◆ leading a team
- ◆ brainstorming
- ◆ chairing a meeting
- ◆ making a speech
- ◆ seminars
- ◆ training sessions
- ◆ job interviews
- ◆ selling a product or service
- ◆ reporting to the board
- ◆ campaign briefing.

Chapter 10

When you have more time

In this Chapter:

◆ **A – Aim: Try to reach the furthest member of the audience.**

◆ **M – Message: Believe in what you're trying to say.**

◆ **B – Benefits: Remember WIIFM.**

◆ **E – Equipment: Rely on your preparation, not on technology.**

◆ **R – Range: Get close enough to make it a two-way process.**

AMBER

In traffic lights, Amber means 'get ready'. In presentations too. The word is an acronym for five essentials in preparing an effective presentation.

A – Aim

Your objective:

What are you trying to achieve?

- to sell
- to persuade
- to inspire
- to motivate
- to inform
- to entertain?

Try to reach the person furthest from your message.

This means the person physically furthest away and also the one who is least interested in your message. Reaching the one who is geographically furthest away means you must project your voice and your conviction with sufficient power to reach and include that person.

However, it is equally important to embrace the one who may be least involved or interested in your topic. To ignore such a member of your audience is not only discourteous, it is downright dangerous. It could result in 'cold spots' in your audience.

A cold spot occurs when one of your listeners is turned off or antagonized. This may arise either because what you are saying is of no interest to that listener, or because you have given offence. The most common cause is not taking sufficient account of your audience. The disconnected listener demonstrates his or her lack of interest or antagonism through negative body language, which soon affects those sitting nearby. Before long, a cluster of four or five people may become switched off, forming a cold spot that is not responding to you.

One cold spot is bad enough. Two or three or more can be devastating. As a speaker you should be alive to the responses of your audience, and if you sense that pockets of listeners are disconnected, you will be thrown off your stride and start to try too hard to switch them on again. Prevention is better than cure, so take the time to research your audience.

Here are some questions you should consider:

- Who will be there?
- How many?
- What level?
- Why do they think they are coming?
- Can they make the decision you want?
- Who knows least about your subject?
- Who might know more than you?

M – Message

Have something (worthwhile) to say.
Ask yourself these 4 questions:

1. What am I trying to achieve?
2. Why should they want to listen to me?
3. What can I offer them that's different and worth having?
4. What do I want at the end of the Presentation?

How to get started:

- Assemble material to serve your objective.
- Get supporting facts for all claims.
- Find out what is being done at present.
- Stay focused: don't try to be comprehensive.
- Believe in what you have to say.

Before you even consider making a presentation you must have something to say, something that is more than the information you are going to impart. It's about what you think about the information. It's what it means to you, and what you want others to think and do about the information or ideas that you want to impart.

Information on its own in neutral. It means very little out of context. Also, the same piece of information may be considered good or bad, according to your point of view. Consider these statements:

> **The Prime Minister has decided to adjust Ministers' salaries to £100,000 a year.**
> *Should they have been higher ... or should we think the figure is too high?*

> **William Hague had been saying that he [Lord Archer] was a man of honour and integrity.** [Max Clifford quoted in *The Guardian*, 16.6.01]
> *Was Max Clifford agreeing or disagreeing with William Hague?*

> **NHS patients now have to wait six weeks for an operation.**
> *Is that up or down on previous waiting times?*

The point of these examples is that the meaning is not clear unless you have the context, or are told whether you are supposed to think well or badly of the news. So it is with any information that goes into your speech or presentation. You may wish to announce that your company's profits have grown by 25 per cent in the past year. But is that good or bad compared with your sector? And what is the consequence of that result? Will your staff be getting a corresponding increase in earnings?

Always answer the 'so what?' question. Imagine your listeners asking, 'Why are you telling me this?' When you make a statement of fact, go on to say, 'Which means that ...' But most importantly, focus on what you want people to remember when they leave. A good way to start is to ask yourself questions like these:

◆ What do I want people to remember about my presentation?
◆ Why should they remember it?
◆ What change do I want to bring about in their thinking, attitudes or behaviour?
◆ How will it benefit them?
◆ Why do I need to tell them about it?

The message must be something that you really want to say. It must belong to you, it must derive from your fund of knowledge and beliefs. The facts and information that you deliver must have passed through your personal filter, so that people understand what you think about them, and why you want to pass them on.

B – Benefits
Remember WIIFM

As every speaker and trainer never tires of saying, everyone's favourite radio station is WII FM, which stands for "What's In It For Me?" Self-interest is the greatest driver. People will listen to you as long as you are offering them something of benefit to themselves. People will do what you ask of them as long as they see how it will benefit them or fit in with whatever is important to them. It may not be of direct benefit to themselves, but it may help a cause or a subject that is close to their hearts, such as a charity or a pet project.

Think of your listeners as carrying a pair of scales. In one pan is their pile of money or their commitment. In the other pan you must place your pile of benefits. Only when your pile of benefits weighs more – substantially more – than their pile of money or commitment, will it seem like a fair exchange to them.

Make a clear distinction between **features** and **benefits**. List all the factual information you wish to include, and alongside each item write its corresponding benefit. Are you recommending a change of lifestyle? Maybe you want to suggest a twenty minute fast walk three times a week. Why? Now here you may want to get a bit technical and talk about the aerobic effect. Well, that's a feature. The benefit is what it enables them to do differently. It may be that they can work longer hours without tiring, or not fall asleep in front of the TV, or have an improved sex life. Those are benefits.

Climate control in a car is a feature. The benefits are greater comfort in either cold or hot and humid conditions, and less likelihood of falling asleep at the wheel on long journeys.

Your speech or presentation is a piece of persuasion. If you have an outcome in mind, if you want to bring about change, you need to be persuasive. That means following the **sequence of persuasion**, which opens with a powerful benefit that grabs the attention of your audience and offers the promise of gain. The subsequent piling on of benefits need to be structured, so that you keep their attention and interest focused, and raise it in a controlled fashion.

Think of the way a direct response advertisement works: it must produce a rapid response by seizing the attention of the target audience, then quickly accelerating interest to the point when the reader decides to buy. The whole process, from a standing start, must be accomplished in a few minutes at most, and often in under one minute. That does not happen by chance. It depends on a carefully planned structured approach that begins with the answers to three vital questions:

◆ What is it?
◆ Is it for me?
◆ How do I get it?

If the benefits are offered in a higgledy-piggledy manner, they may cancel each other out and stall the quickening pulse of desire. Similarly, a speech or presentation needs a shape as well as a sequence, with benefits coming in a steady stream rather than as an avalanche, and offered through the controlled tension of making a claim then proving it. The claim raises expectations; the proof provides the satisfaction.

E – Equipment

Rely on your preparation, not on technology
- be well-informed
- be rehearsed
- only visual aids that support your case
- don't hide behind technology:
- what if it breaks down?

This point concerns more than the hardware you might use: it concerns **your own readiness** for the event. How well equipped are you? Examine your own expertise and ask yourself how much you know about the subject on which you are going to speak. <u>Are you the expert or are you delivering someone else's expertise?</u>

Many a speaker starts by rummaging in the works of others, on the grounds that to borrow from one person is plagiarism, but borrowing from several is research. It is certainly all right to research your topic, but do ensure that you make the information part of your own belief system before you attempt to impart it to others, or you will find yourself trying to remember what you read instead of what you know.

The next step is to ensure that you **properly prepared**. To be properly equipped, you need the right message, a planned structure and all the necessary back-up information.

Now consider **how** you will deliver your message. Will you stand and deliver without visual aids? Or will you use any of the usual equipment? If you are proposing to use PowerPoint, for example, do you have a back-up plan should the laptop or projector malfunction, or if the fuse blows? Are you able to present with a flip chart alone? If you are using overheads, either as first choice or as back-up, have you practised your presentation so that you can move from each overhead to the next without losing your flow?

If you intend to use **multi-media,** you must rehearse in front of people who will give you good feedback, especially as to whether you come across as the main attraction ... or as an acolyte to what comes up on the screen.

Have you considered whether to prepare **handouts** – and are they ready? To print the right number of handouts you must obviously know how many people will be there. And you need to plan to be there early enough to place them on every seat, if your intention is to give out in advance, or to finish early enough to circulate them after your talk.

It is a good idea to **write your own introduction** and send it in advance to the person who will be introducing you. But don't rely on that alone. Take a printed copy to the event and hand it to your introducer, saying: 'I've prepared my own introduction, to make it easier for you. It would really help to set the scene if you would read it as it stands.'

Finally, check that all the hardware equipment works, (including an extension lead if you are using a laptop) then rehearse and time each section.

R – Range

Get close enough to make it a two-way process

Even though you are the only one actually speaking, the communication process must be two-way if it is to be successful. The essential ingredients of that process are:

- Spoken language
- Body language
- Eye contact
- Vocal technique
- Pace and pauses
- Gestures and movement.

Language

Understand the difference between written and spoken language, and never speak as though you were reading a written text, or you will risk losing the attention of your listeners very soon. With rare exceptions, speeches and presentations should be delivered in language not too far from the way you would speak to interested friends in your local pub. The exceptions are those charismatic motivational speakers or political leaders whose passion is often matched by powerful oratory, vivid word pictures and language that reaches deep into the hearts of their hearers.

For most of us, however, the advice is more prosaic. Avoid jargon or anything too technical that forces your listeners to stop and work out the meaning. Make it easy for them to know where you are heading with your thoughts, and to understand its relevance to them.

Body language

Become aware of the messages that we all communicate through our posture, stance, facial expressions and involuntary twitches. Consider your own as well as the messages you can learn to read from those in front of you.

Your communication with the audience begins the moment they first set eyes on you. And because you never get a second chance to make a first impression, always try to make that first impression a powerful one. Stand erect, be open and have a ready smile. Let them like you.

When you speak, <u>move with a purpose</u>, not like a caged tiger. Notice that your listeners' body language falls into two categories: **voluntary** and **involuntary**. Voluntary signs include smiling and nodding, or frowning and shaking of the heads. Involuntary signs include a tilt of the head (not sure), knitting eyebrows (don't agree), folded arms (resistance), vacant stare (disconnected).

If you are getting negative signals, it's time for a change of pace.

Eye contact

Sweep your audience, making sure that everyone gets **3 seconds of eye contact** from time to time. When listeners break off eye contact with you, they are probably uncomfortable with what you are saying. Conversely, if you do not hold eye contact with them, or miss them out altogether, they will feel left out. Remember to include those sitting close to you, including the meeting chairman, and those out of your normal line of sight.

Eye contact plays a major part in your two-way communication.

Vocal technique
Speak with sufficient volume and conviction to reach and embrace the people at the farthest corners of the room. Some people deliberately sit at the back and around the corner in order to avoid committing themselves to whatever is going on.

By filling the room with your voice and your presence, you will engage their attention. By using vocal variety and altering your pace from time to time you will retain their interest. Don't be afraid to pause – apart from the dramatic effect it can have, it helps your listeners to take in what you have just said.

Gestures and movement
Gestures can enhance your message, but they can also be distracting. Some speakers merely beat time with their hands, and that can be irritating. Use your gestures to illustrate your points, because you are the most significant visual aid. Use large gestures, and practise them in front of a mirror so that you develop attractive, rhythmic movements.

When you pace about, your movements are seen as expressions of your own unease. But when you move with a purpose, matching your movements to your message, you enhance your meaning, and strengthen your connection with your audience.

Come out from behind the lectern, approach your audience if you can, but do not overwhelm those closest to you. Let it be a natural process, like leaning forward when you have something significant or personal to say.

In summary ...

In conclusion, the word to remember is AMBER:

1. **AIM at the furthest member of your audience.**
2. **Always have a MESSAGE and believe in it.**
3. **Focus on BENEFITS not facts or features.**
4. **EQUIP yourself through preparation, not machinery.**
5. **Get in RANGE for two-way communication.**

AMBER for Professional Presentations

Chapter 11

Checklist

In this Chapter:

Points to bear in mind for each ingredient of your speech, including:

◆ **type of speech**
◆ **objective**
◆ **audience**
◆ **occasion**
◆ **hook**
◆ **message**
◆ **benefits**
◆ **structure**
◆ **outcome**
◆ **visual aids**
◆ **equipment / facilities**
◆ **notes**
◆ **delivery**

TYPE OF SPEECH

- Persuasive
- Informative
- Motivational
- Entertaining
- Event-related.

OBJECTIVE

- Why are you making the speech?
- What change do you want to bring about?
- What outcome do you want?
- What's the least you will settle for?
- How will you know if they agree to it?

AUDIENCE

- Who will be there – age, seniority, knowledge of your subject?
- How many?
- Why are they coming – do they have to?
- What are their expectations likely to be?
- What will be their attitude to you?

OCCASION

- Is it business or private?
- Does your speech have to be related to the occasion?
- Formal or informal?
- Why is it you giving the speech?

HOOK

- ◆ What will grab their attention?
- ◆ What will they be surprised to hear?
- ◆ Is it relevant to your topic?
- ◆ Will it make a vivid picture in their minds?

MESSAGE

- ◆ What is it you have to say?
- ◆ Do you really want to say it – and why?
- ◆ How is it different from what others have said?
- ◆ How will it benefit the audience?
- ◆ What's *your* contribution to the subject?
- ◆ Which principal benefit can you express in the title?
- ◆ How would you like your speech to be summarized later?
- ◆ Which ONE idea can change their thinking on the subject?
- ◆ Will it matter if you never made the speech?

BENEFITS

- ◆ Remember WII FM: what's in it for me?
- ◆ The Hook grabs attention, but benefits retain it.
- ◆ Translate features into their corresponding benefits.
- ◆ Your pile of benefits must outweigh the cost of acceptance.
- ◆ Benefits appeal to the heart as well as the head.
- ◆ Facts tell, feelings sell.

STRUCTURE

- Use the Rule of Threes.
- Adopt one of the simple structures to develop each argument.
- Those structures can provide the overall framework too.
- It simplifies your preparation.
- It helps maintain a balanced content.
- Slot each idea or argument into place on the structured template.
- Rely on the structure to keep you on track.
- Helps your audience to understand and follow you.
- Most useful structures are:
  - Past / Present / Future
  - Problem / Cause / Solution
  - PREP 1 (Position / Reason / Example / Position)
  - PREP 2 (Proposition / Reason / Example / Proposition)
  - Cause / Effect / Proposal
  - AIDA (Attention / Interest / Desire / Action)
  - Tell x 3.

OUTCOME

- Always start with the end in view.
- What do you want to happen after you speak?
- How should your listeners show they agree with you?
- What action do you want them to take?
- How can you make the change permanent?
- What should happen immediately?
- What should change in the longer term?
- What feedback would you like after you have spoken?

VISUAL AIDS

- They must support but not supplant the speaker.
- Do not try to illustrate everything you say.
- If you are using slides, keep them to a minimum.
- If you can make your point without a slide, do so.
- For slide content follow the 5 x 5 rule (max. 7 x 7).
- If using a flip chart, write letters 2 inches high.
- Do not use a flip chart for audiences of more than 25 people.
- Always check that visual aids can be seen by everyone.
- When writing on flip charts or whiteboards, do not turn your back.
- Use pictures whenever possible.
- Visual aids must be legitimate summaries of what you are saying.

EQUIPMENT / FACILITIES

- Will there be a platform or podium for speakers?
- Microphone? Stand or lapel?
- Lectern?
- Can you move about?
- Flip chart?
- Back screen for projector?
- Full or half lighting?
- Can you be seen from every seat? (Check it yourself)

NOTES

- Notes should not be read.
- Use headings and bullet points whenever possible.
- Feel free to pick up your notes and hold them in your hand.
- Raise them to eye level, don't drop your head.
- Use cards for preference: number them.
- A4 sheets are acceptable.
- A mind map is best.

DELIVERY

- Develop the right speaking voice.
- Use vocal variety.
- Project your voice to reach everyone in the room.
- Speak with conviction.
- Practise impromptu speaking, using the structures given.

In summary ...

1. **Refer to the Checklist whenever preparing a speech or presentation, to remind yourself of the important considerations affecting each of the ingredients.**

2. **Arrive early and check the layout, equipment and facilities.**

3. **Follow the outline above to prepare your first draft in just 15 minutes.**

CHECKLIST FOR THE 15-MINUTE PREPARATION

- State your **Theme.**
- Write Your **Title**
  - must express the Theme.
- What's Your **CORE MESSAGE?**
  - what do you want to say about your Theme?
  [1 minute]

- Brainstorm **Ideas** on the Theme
  - don't filter: let the ideas flow.
  [6 minutes]

- Write Your **Outline**
  - use established **Structures.**
  PREP/ Past, Present, Future / Problem, Cause
  Solution / Tell x 3.
- Number your Brainstormed Ideas in the order in
  which to use them, fitting in with your Structure.
  [2 minutes]

- Rewrite the Ideas, in the chosen Structure, under
  appropriate **Headings** and **Sub-heads.**
- Refine as **speaker's notes** – This is your FIRST
  DRAFT.
  [6 minutes]

Finally:
- **Speak** the speech into a tape recorder, following the
  notes.
- **Re-write the CORE MESSAGE.**
- **Summarize** the whole speech in a single sentence.

About the Author

Phillip Khan-Panni is a Speaker, Trainer and Writer, and a consultant on marketing and managing customer relationships.

In competitive public speaking, he is the most successful speaker in Britain, holding three major records: seven times UK Champion, three times Anglo-Irish Champion, and the first speaker from Britain to win the Silver Medal in the World Championships of public speaking.

As a professional speaker he speaks about effective communication, cross-cultural awareness, and marketing issues such as Customer Relationship Management and Direct Marketing. He is regarded as the foremost authority in Britain on precise and concise communication.

Through his consultancies, PKP Communicators and 4C International, he coaches senior business executives in public speaking, presentation skills and cross-cultural communication, both in the UK and abroad. One of his clients said, 'Don't ever speak in public without first speaking to Phillip.'

He has a business background in direct marketing, sales management, newspapers and magazines. With one sales force that he managed, he tripled revenue in his first year. He is a Founder Director of the Professional Speakers Association, with responsibility for marketing, and past Chairman of the Croydon and East Surrey branch of the Chartered Institute of Marketing.

He is the author of *2-4-6-8, How Do You Communicate?*, a companion volume in this series.

Contact Details
You can contact Phillip at:
PKP Communicators
35 Hillbrow Road
Bromley, Kent BR1 4JL
Telephone: 07000 SPEAKS (773257)
E-mail: pkp@mainspeaker.com

Further Reading from How To Books

2-4-6-8 How Do You Communicate?, Phillip Khan-Panni, 2001.

A to Z of Correct English, Angela Burt, 2000.

How to Talk to the Media, Judith Byrne, 2000.

Increase Your Word Power, Angela Burt, 2001.

Making an After Dinner Speech, John Bowden, 2nd edition, 2001.

Making Great Presentations, Ghassan Hasbani, 1999.

Say it with Pictures, Dr Harry Alder, 2001.

Toasts & Short Speeches, John Bowden, 2000.

Writing, Speaking, Listening, Helen Wilkie, 2001.

For comprehensive information on How To Books' titles visit How To Books on-line at www.howtobooks.co.uk